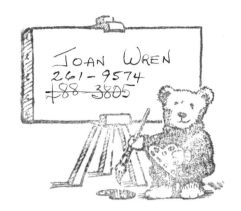

JOAN WREN
261-9574
~~788-3805~~

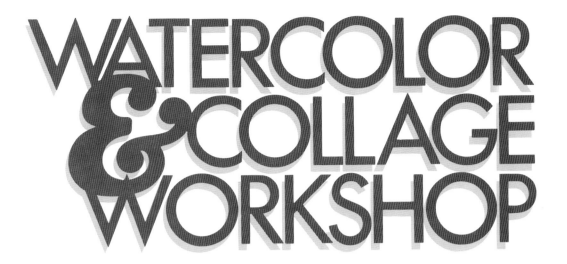

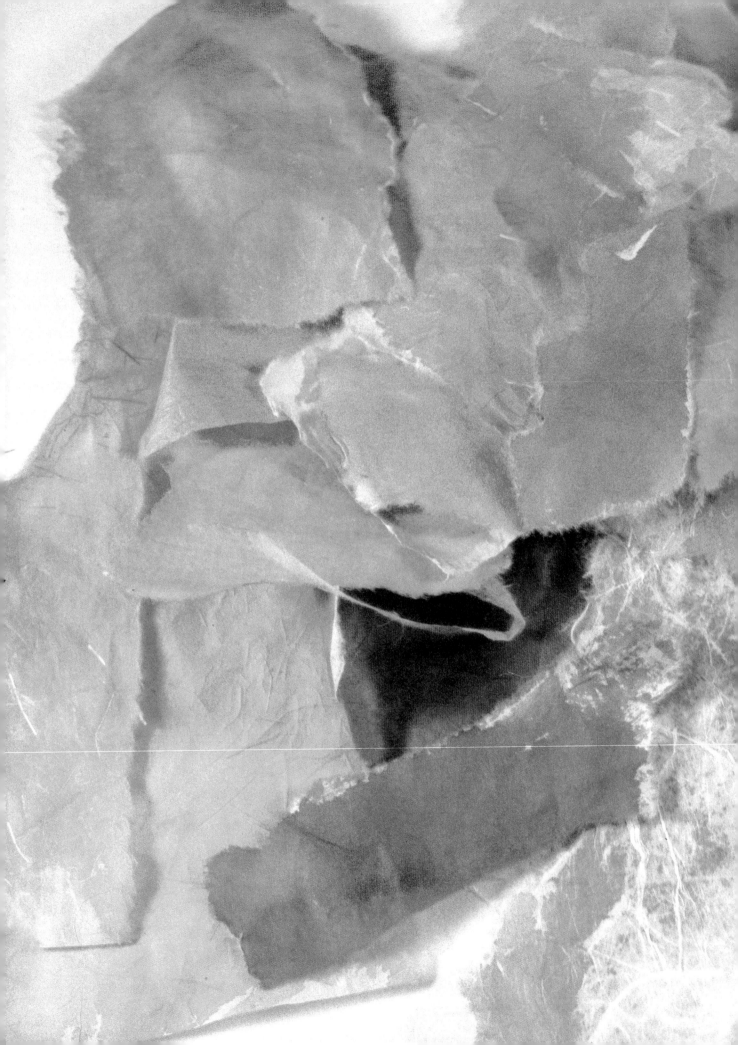

WATERCOLOR & COLLAGE WORKSHOP

GERALD BROMMER

WATSON-GUPTILL PUBLICATIONS/NEW YORK

To Dorothy Bowman and Richard Challis, whose professional abilities
and skills have encouraged and enabled me to pursue my career
as an artist. Their early interest in the watercolor and collage
process fostered my desire to explore the medium over many years.
They are good and true friends.

First published 1986 in the United States and Canada
by Watson-Guptill Publications,
a division of Billboard Publications, Inc.,
1515 Broadway, New York, N.Y. 10036

Library of Congress Cataloging-in-Publication Data
Brommer, Gerald, 1927–
   Watercolor and collage workshop.
   Includes index.
   1. Watercolor painting—Technique.   2. Collage—
Technique.   I. Title.
ND2420.B73   1986   702'.8'12   86-1322
ISBN 0-8230-5652-X

Distributed in the United Kingdom by Phaidon Press Ltd.,
Littlegate House, St. Ebbe's St., Oxford

Printed in Singapore

3   4   5   6   7   8   9   /   90

ACKNOWLEDGMENTS

Every book is a cooperative enterprise, requiring the skills of many people before it is completed. Although authors seem to get most of the credit, they usually do only a part of the work. I want to thank Mary Suffudy, senior editor for Watson-Guptill Publications, for suggesting that I write the book and for continuing to have faith in the project, and Susan Heinemann, also at Watson-Guptill, for her sensitive editing of the text. I wish I could personally thank all the skilled people on the publication staff whom I have never met and who never receive much credit: editors, book designers, layout and pasteup artists, typographers, and production personnel. Their individual contributions have made this book a reality.

I am indebted to the twenty-four artists who consented to have their work reproduced in various parts of the book, and to Mary Carroll Nelson who put me in touch with many of them. The time they took to verbalize their thoughts and techniques add greatly to the content of the book. Their generosity will help make all of us better artists.

I am also indebted to the hundreds of students who enthusiastically delved into the collage and watercolor processes in my workshops. Their creativity and ability to adapt to new techniques continually encouraged me to share these ideas with other artists.

I also want to thank the many art dealers and gallery owners who encouraged me over the past twenty years to continue working with the collage process and who ultimately had to carefully explain it to their clients. Among them are Barbara Beretich, Dorothy Bowman, Richard Challis, Arvilla Huney, Louis Newman, Richard Spencer, Pat Weaver, Esther Wells, Judith Williams, and Chuck Winter. Without their faith and help, the process would not have been seen by the public.

And to my wife, Georgia, a huge thank you. We gave up a vacation in England so the manuscript could be finished on time. Her constant encouragement is a true and continuing blessing in my life.

CONTENTS

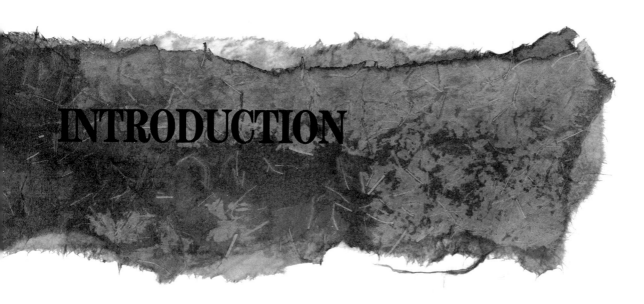

INTRODUCTION

Collage is much more than a technique. As this book emphasizes, it can be a way of learning about how paintings are constructed. Regardless of the medium you choose, the basic processes in painting remain the same: designing and composing, determining values and colors, and varying edges to provide boundaries or allow passage. Collage can help you become more aware of these processes and refine your skills. By experimenting with collage, you may become a more proficient painter, better able to express yourself visually.

As you tear and add shapes and textures to your work, you are encouraged to observe the shapes and textures of nature. The idea, however, is not to duplicate what you see. As artists, we are free to alter what we see to create paintings. Because the collage process emphasizes changes during the working process, it may help you perceive more clearly the abstract qualities of nature, which can contribute to more effective painting.

This book adopts an exploratory attitude toward painting, involving trial and error, experimentation, and a questioning approach. Although the focus is on the combination of watercolor and collage, many of the lessons can be applied to other media. The ultimate goal is to encourage you to loosen up your approach to painting, to explore alternative avenues of expression, and to try new techniques and methods of saying what you wish to say—in whatever medium you choose.

As you explore new processes, try to do so with a spirit of adventure, to see where they will take you. Do not feel that every work must be of gallery or exhibition quality. When you use new materials, take time to see what is happening, to observe the interaction of various media and papers. Do not force these trial pieces to match a "picture" you visualized when you started. Keep in mind that this is a learning process—and allow yourself to learn. Finished visual statements can come later, after a period of exploration.

The question is often asked: If you use collage in the work, is it still a watercolor? An exhibition committee may provide an answer, but that should not concern you. Regardless of the medium, style, or subject matter, art as visual expression should not be regulated by rules. We should use whatever materials we need to make good paintings. Our goal as artists is to communicate and make the best paintings possible. If we must add collage to make our statements more convincing and complete, we should not hesitate to do so. That does not mean we should not try to make a superb transparent watercolor or acrylic painting, it simply means that at times we may want to make something different—something that allows us to express ourselves in a unique and personal way.

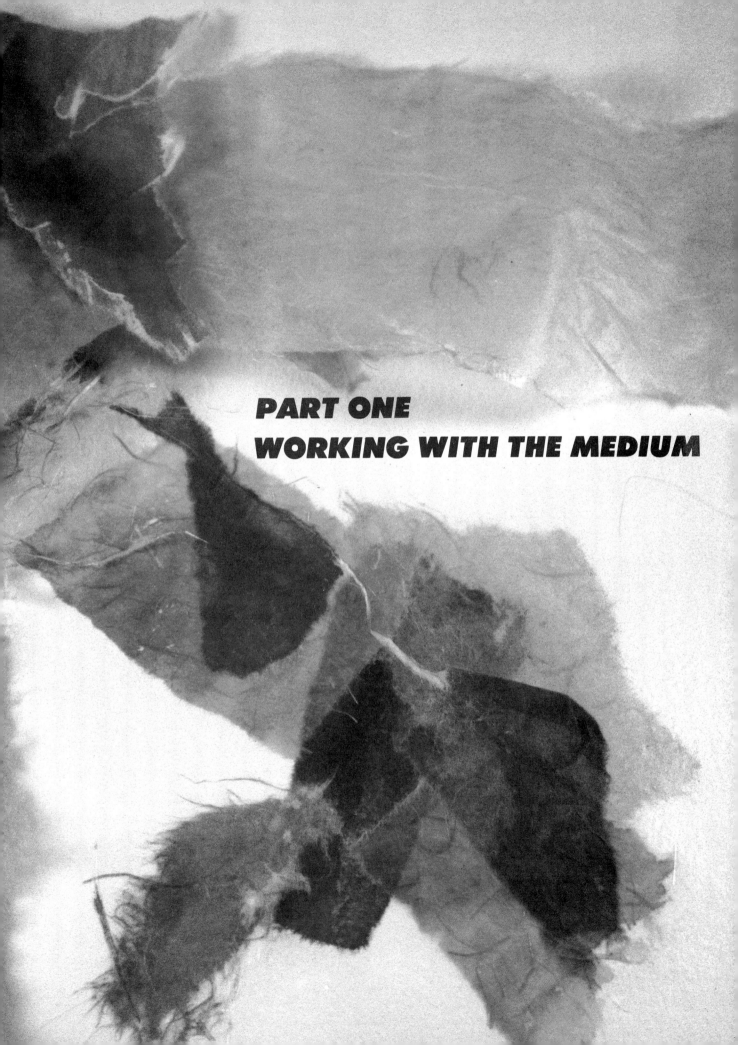

PART ONE
WORKING WITH THE MEDIUM

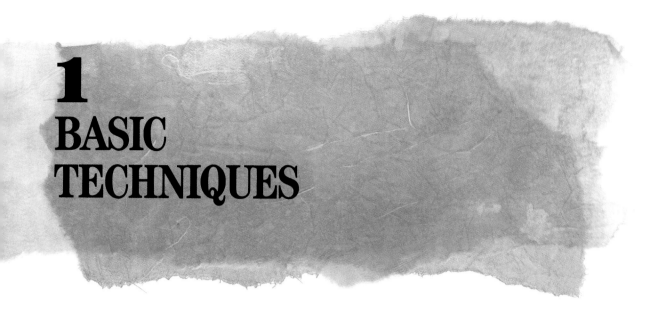

1 BASIC TECHNIQUES

Since Pablo Picasso and Georges Braque first began adding collaged materials to their paintings in 1912, artists have explored the process in countless ways. All kinds of paper, cloth, wood, plastic, and metal have been adhered to surfaces of paper, cardboard, canvas, and Masonite. Not only has collage been combined with almost every painting medium, but it has also been used alone—without paint of any kind.

The French called the pasting technique developed by the Cubists *papier collé*, which simply means "pasted paper." The Anglicized term *collage* refers to the process of pasting paper to a surface. To artists, the term implies selection, skill, and sensitivity in using paper materials and adhesives. A collage can take on many meanings, depending on the past experiences and current purposes of the artist using the materials.

This book focuses on the process of adhering papers to watercolor surfaces to provide a textured ground for paint-

ing. Although the collaged papers may stand on their own as part of the painting structure, generally the collage process is used here to create exciting and sensuous surfaces, with the collaged papers almost losing their identities for the sake of a unified painting.

As a rule of thumb, collage should be used only when the process helps to improve your painting, enhancing the surface and making the painting more exciting. It is counterproductive to attach papers to a surface if this causes confusion and creates unnecessary problems. Always remember, however, that your responsibility as an artist is to make the best paintings possible and to articulate your feelings and impressions through visual means, using paint on paper. Take advantage of every available resource to help you fully communicate your ideas and concepts. Only by exploring the possibilities of collage can you determine if this method will enhance your work.

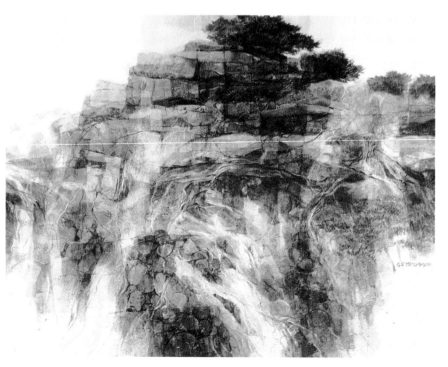

COASTAL IMPRESSION. Watercolor and collage, 22" x 30" (56 x 76 cm). Collection of Mr. Harry Holt.

An imaginary coastal scene derived from several studies, this painting is constructed on a richly textured ground of Oriental papers. The textures of rocks and rushing water dominate the surface, which is woven together with vertical and horizontal lines and contrasting colors and values.

MATERIALS AND TOOLS

Collage implies working with materials of various kinds. This book focuses on the use of transparent watercolor, Oriental (rice) papers, and white glue in a variety of combinations. You are encouraged, however, to try any other material that might seem useful in developing your own personal visual vocabulary.

PAINTS AND BRUSHES

When combining watercolor and collage, use the same paints as for a transparent watercolor painting. Although any watercolor brush can be employed effectively with this combination technique, flat brushes are best for the initial application of paint to collaged surfaces. Choose flat softhair brushes (sable, synthetic, or a combination) in ½-, ¾-, or 1-inch widths, depending on the size of your work.

Later, as you develop your own techniques and style, you may select a pointed brush, in any size. While sable brushes work very well on collaged surfaces, the abrasive textures can rapidly wear down the delicate pointed tips (flags). Brushes with combinations of hairs (sable and synthetic, for example) are therefore far more economical.

ADHESIVES

Basic to the collage process is an adhesive to hold papers to the surface. There are many glues, pastes, waxes, and adhesives that stick paper to paper. In working with watercolor and collage, however, the adhesive material must work *with* the water-based media, not fight it. In general, waxy materials should be eliminated, as they resist applications of watercolor.

Two products seem to work well with watercolor: white PVA (polyvinyl acetate) glue and acrylic matte medium. Do not, however, use these materials full-strength. Both need to be diluted with water to provide surfaces that accept watercolor without resistance. Although other adhesives have certain desirable properties, they may be more difficult to work with (extended drying time and resolubility, for example). However, you are encouraged to experiment!

Clear, plastic cups work well as containers for your glue and for the water needed to dilute it. A piece of cardboard makes an excellent disposable surface, on which the glue and water can be mixed to desired consistencies.

Brushes for applying glue should be firm enough to control both the glue and the paper. Bristle brushes, flats or brights, in ¼-inch to ½-inch sizes (numbers 6–8, for example) are most useful. Because PVA glue and acrylic medium dry to rocklike hardness, be sure to clean your brushes thoroughly in warm water immediately after use. If you forget, hold the dried brush under the hot water faucet for a minute or two, or soak it in hot water for several minutes until flexible.

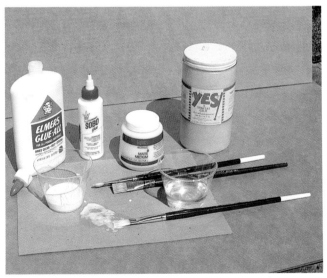

Many kinds of adhesives will stick paper to paper, but diluted acrylic medium or white glue works best for the processes described in this book. At times Yes! glue may be helpful in sticking pieces of heavy watercolor paper (300 lb. for example) or papers other than the Oriental handmade varieties to the surface. Use a stiff bristle brush to mix the glue and water to a desired consistency and apply it to the painting surface.

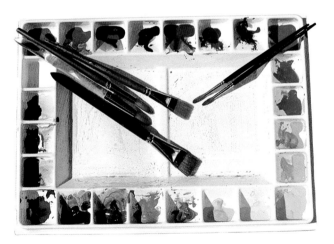

Your regular complement of watercolor brushes (flats and rounds) and current palette of colors are all that you need for the painting process described later. Bear in mind that, because the collaged surface is somewhat abrasive, synthetic brushes will outlast sables.

This selection of white Oriental papers is laid out on a dark background. Note the variations in thickness, opacity, and fiber content. (The more opaque papers are lighter in value in this photograph.) Observe, for instance, the difference between the two Unryu papers in the first and second rows. The three lace papers (lower right) represent only a few of the patterns available.

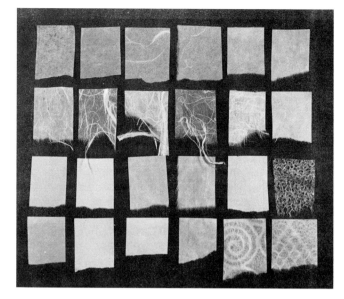

There are not as many natural-colored papers as white papers, but the textural variety is just as great. When seen against a dark background sheet, the most opaque papers generally appear lightest in value. Note the different characteristics of the two Kasuiri papers in the second row.

Kinwashi Natural	Kinwashi	Kasuri	Yunglong	A.K. Toyama
Kasuiri	Kasuiri	Chiri	Kitikata	Bunko
Okawara	Mitsumi Natural	Kochi	Sekishu	Gampi Torinoko Natural

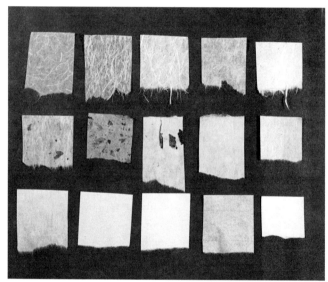

The same papers are shown on a light table, which emphasizes the types of fibers. The more opaque papers allow less light to pass through them and therefore appear darker here.

Gasen Kyoto	Gampi Gasen	Yoroshi	Unryu	Kozo Gasen	Mulberry
Horuki Miya	Horuki Light	Horuki Heavy	Unryu	Nippon	Natsume
Kozo Heavy	Torinoko	Suzuki	Kozo Light	Iyo Glazed	Lace
Goyu	Masa	Gampi Torinoko White	Moriko	Lace	Lace

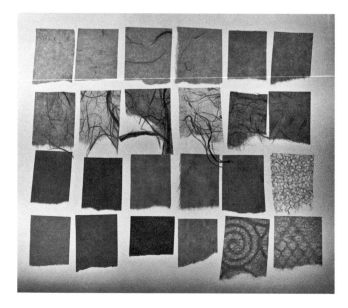

GROUNDS

Grounds are the surfaces on which paintings are made. Watercolors, for example, are usually painted on paper. For a collage, the ground should be sturdier than the papers applied to it. The heavier the collage materials are, the heavier the support should be. While excellent collages have been made on stretched 140 lb. papers, it is a decided advantage to use 300 lb. or heavier paper, which need not be stretched. Watercolor boards also make fine collage supports, as do mounted papers.

For the techniques described in this book, rough paper is best, because its texture is most compatible with that of Oriental papers. When smooth papers (cold- or hot-pressed) or illustration boards are used, there is a distracting textural difference between the Oriental papers and the supporting ground. All the demonstrations in this book are carried out on Arches 300 lb. rough paper (unless otherwise noted), but you are encouraged to experiment with other grounds.

ORIENTAL PAPERS

Most of the papers used as collage materials in this book are handmade papers from Japan. Commonly called "rice papers," these sheets are mostly made from five basic fibers: kozo, gampi, mitsumata, sulphite, and manila. Varying combinations of these fibers, plus a few additives, produce the scores of decorative, textural sheets on the market.

Oriental papers are long-fibered and difficult to tear, making them ideal for printmaking. Many are acid-free, and most are highly absorbent. Their other characteristics range from completely opaque to nearly transparent, from thick to thin, from white to neutral to black, from smooth to highly textured, from inexpensive to costly. Since the papers are handmade, however, the quality and composition may vary from one maker to another. Papers with the same name, purchased from different suppliers, may differ noticeably in their characteristics.

The sizes of the papers are almost as variable as their content. Most are about 24 × 36 inches (61 × 91 cm), but many are smaller and a few are larger. When ordering, note the sizes, so as to avoid disappointment when the sheets arrive at your studio.

The illustrations show how some of these papers look. There are many more than those pictured here, but a basic supply of six to ten papers will provide a great variety of texture. It is best to stick with white and neutral papers, since it is difficult to alter the hue of colored Oriental papers with watercolor. When papers have alternate smooth and textured sides, they should be collaged so the textured (absorbent) side is up. Most papers, however, are about as absorbent on one side as the other.

All the papers have Japanese names, which may be difficult to remember. It is helpful to write the names on small samples and keep them for reference and reordering. A list of ten basic papers might include: Chiri, Kasuri, Kinwashi (heavy), Kinwashi (white), Natsume, Unryu (or Yoroshi), Mulberry, Kasuiri, Okawara, and Horuki. The choice, however, is a personal one, and it will take some time to arrive at your own basic selection of papers. I have purposely not mentioned the names of papers in the demonstrations, so that you will feel free to explore on your own.

PAPER SOURCES

If you have a paper source in your city, you can choose your papers by feeling them and noting their opacity and textural characteristics. If art supply stores do not stock Oriental papers, try shops in Asian neighborhoods or Oriental specialty stores. If no ready supply is available to you, you may write to one of the following suppliers. All have samples, some in book form and others assorted in envelopes, which will be sent for a fee.

Daniel Smith Inc., 4130 First Avenue South, Seattle, WA 98134

New York Central Supply Co., 62 Third Avenue, New York, NY 10003

Nikko Natural Fabrics, PO Box 71, Kamuela, HI 96743

Japan Folk Art, 147 Monte Rey Drive South, Los Alamos, NM 87544

Aiko's, 714 North Wabash Avenue, Chicago, IL 60611

Paper Source, 1506 West 12th Street, Los Angeles, CA 90015

No single source carries all the papers available, since there are simply too many varieties and variations. Obtain several catalogs to ensure the widest possible selection. Do not fall in love with any particular paper, because it may be discontinued.

Collagists often swap papers with each other to increase the variety of textures in each of their studios. If you or your friends make handmade papers, these may also be included in your palette of collage papers. Collect examples of white and natural-colored papers and note their source, availability, and possible uses.

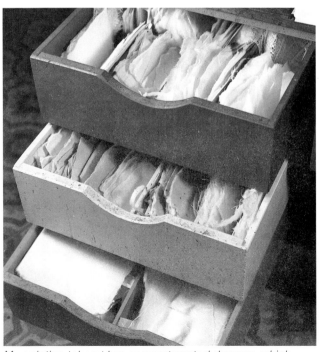

My painting taboret has compartmented drawers, which contain torn Oriental papers of various types, arranged according to opacity, texture, and color. When I begin a collage, I select my papers and place them alongside the painting, to be retorn and applied as needed.

THE BENEFITS OF
A TEXTURED GROUND

The ultimate reason for choosing any technique is to make a better painting—a more complete visual statement. Adding textured papers to your working surface provides an excellent opportunity to develop exquisite textural effects. If your goal in a particular painting is to interpret and express the textural qualities of things around you, this process can prove valuable. Or if you wish to explore texture for its own sake, as a painting expression, then combining watercolor and collage is a practical and exciting technique. By adding five or more kinds of textured paper to your painting surface, you can eliminate much of your concern about developing appropriate textures with brushstrokes.

To remain fresh and creative in their approach, artists need the stimulation of diverse working methods. The watercolor and collage technique provides an alternative to wet-in-wet and drybrush techniques. It also provides an alternative to hot- and cold-pressed and rough surfaces. With the addition of collaged papers, you can build varied surfaces that are visually stimulating and exciting to use. If you are searching for new and challenging directions in your painting, watercolor and collage may be the perfect technique for you.

Because the collage process involves the reintroduction of whites in the form of opaque papers, it gives you greater freedom to design the surface while painting. Visual movement, transitions, balance, pattern, emphasis, and contrast can be developed initially, but they can also be altered, adjusted, and strengthened as the painting progresses. This flexibility can help you to understand and master the principles of design as you work.

Moreover, by collaging Oriental papers, you can perform major surgery on paintings that do not meet your own standards of excellence. Unsuccessful paintings can often be reclaimed by collaging the surface with textured papers. You may choose to repair only a small area, or redesign and repaint the entire work. For the artist who craves the opportunity to salvage a painting that has gone wrong, the collage process can be invaluable.

Most important, watercolor and collage can free artists from the restrictions of traditional approaches to painting and permit them to handle their brushes and paints in loose and expressive ways. After the basics of the medium are understood, personal expression can be free and direct. Working with collage encourages on-the-spot evaluation and interpretation. It makes you more aware of what is happening on the painting surface and compels you to react to the surface as the painting develops.

These benefits carry over to transparent watercolor painting itself. After trying collage, painters who use watercolor exclusively usually find themselves more direct and confident in their approaches to painting, more apt to experiment and innovate as they construct their watercolors, and better able to react to what happens in a painting as it develops.

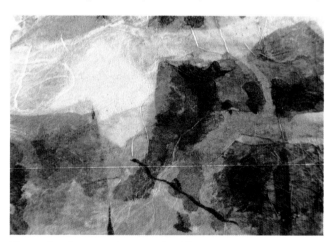
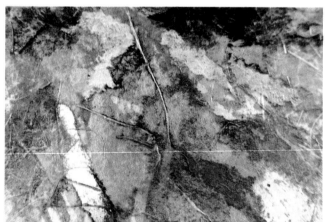

These details were photographed from a group of small, abstract watercolor and collage paintings. They typify the kinds of textural surfaces possible with this technique.

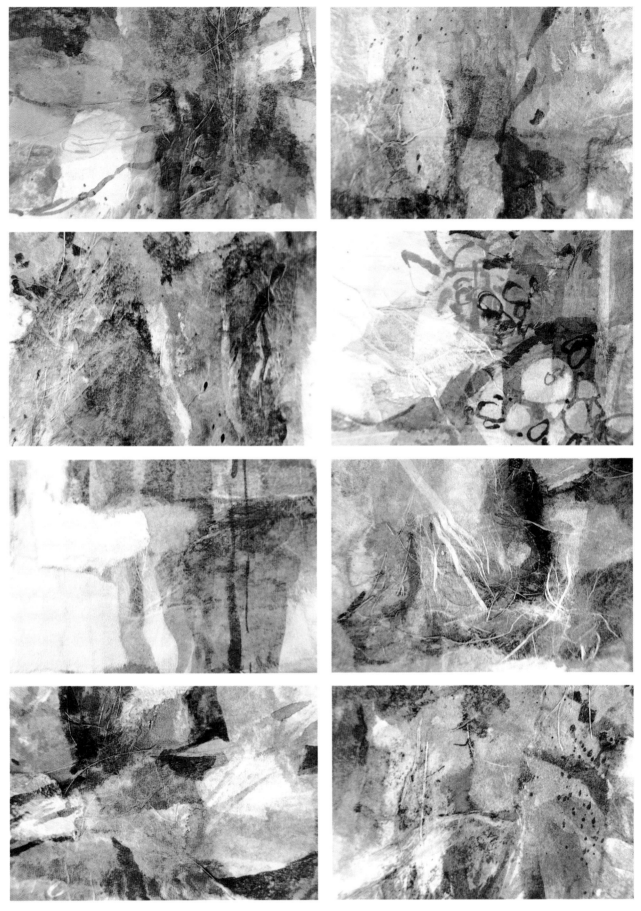

THE BASIC LAYERING PROCESS

There are many variations to the layering process with water-color and collage, but this exercise introduces the fundamental techniques. After these basic steps are understood and mastered, you can begin to explore the possibilities of the medium in the context of your own work. To concentrate on the process, it is important that you eliminate subject matter from your first collages. If you try to make trees, barns, or rocks, you will miss much of what happens in the layering process. Getting acquainted with the medium is the goal here. Working with abstract designs will make it possible for you to concentrate on texture, layering, and painting processes. The following procedure underlies all the watercolor and collage demonstrations in this book.

Begin by cutting a half-sheet of 300 lb. watercolor paper into six squares, each about 7½ × 7½ inches (19 × 19 cm). There is nothing magical about the size, except that six squares can be cut from a half-sheet of paper without any leftover scraps. For most landscape painters, squares work best for developing abstract images because rectangles immediately suggest objective landscapes. Since childhood, we have been encouraged to "draw the horizon line first" on a blank piece of rectangular paper. On a square sheet, there is no such unseen landscape orientation.

A design concept called bridging is useful in establishing a directional orientation. Visual movement will emanate from an area of emphasis created by intersecting two bridges, one generally horizontal and the other vertical. Complete a series of sketches to familiarize yourself with the bridging concept (see the sketches here). Make your bridges go to the edges of the paper to involve the entire sheet in the design.

After the feeling of bridging is established in your sketches, begin painting similar designs on the squares of paper. Use a limited palette so color mixing does not become a dominant feature. Also, in the beginning, restrict yourself to light and middle values. Bear in mind that extra-heavy pigment can cause glue to discolor when the collaging process begins. Paint all six squares and allow them to dry.

Now select five or more kinds of Oriental paper (the more you use, the more exciting the result). Tear each sheet into pieces about 2 × 4 inches (5 × 10 cm). When you begin to collage, tear off pieces about ½ × 1 inch (1 × 2 cm) and glue them to the painted surface. Use a ½-inch bristle brush to apply the glue mixture to the painted surface. Place the torn paper on the glued area and use the same brush to flatten the edges and to adhere the paper firmly to the ground.

Because the edges and fibers of the torn paper will show up in later color layering, place the collaged pieces to help direct the eye to the center of interest. Try distributing the pieces of paper on the surface to balance the textures. Overlay two pieces of paper to create a third, layered texture. Leave the four corners of the square blank, but have some fibered papers act as transitions between the painted and unpainted areas. On several squares, you may decide to leave some painted areas uncollaged, while on other squares all the painted areas will be covered with textured papers. Allow the collage to dry completely.

All the steps up to this point have been aimed simply at preparing a ground for painting. The actual painting will be done on the textured, collaged surface. Of course, some color from the initial painted layer may show through the collaged layer. Some of these areas may not even require additional painting.

Because the collaged surface is not as absorbent as either the 300 lb. watercolor paper or the Oriental papers glued to it, it is necessary to use a drybrush technique when applying color. Dip a flat brush in a watercolor wash and then partially dry it by touching it to a tissue or a paint rag. Now explore several techniques. First, caress the paper with the brush. Then brush firmly. Next scumble and scrub. With each technique you try, carefully observe what is happening on the collaged sheets. Become aware of subtle color changes as the color comes in contact with several kinds of paper—some more absorbent and differently textured than others.

Experiment further. Paint one wash over another. The colors beneath the collage layer will emerge with the overpainting. Colors can gradually be intensified and darks can be added where necessary. Do not simply apply the same color on top of the collaged papers as you have used below them.

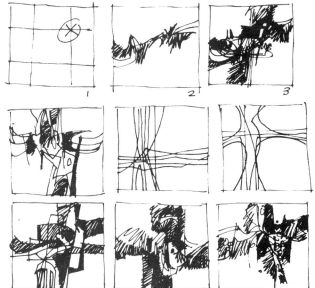

Use design sketches such as these to remind you about the arrangement and placement of visual elements in your work. Sketch 1 suggests a method for locating the center of interest. Sketch 2 illustrates the first step in bridging space. Sketch 3 shows the finished bridging concept. The remaining sketches explore different bridging possibilities.

Complementary colors may be interesting, but even slight changes in hue can emphasize the textural surface. Warms over cools and cools over warms can be visually stimulating. If colors are too intense, or if water begins to form puddles, blot with absorbent tissue or a paint rag.

Allow the collaged surface to suggest the placement of color and line. Make soft edges and hard edges. Use a pointed brush to add linear passages. Read the developing painting and respond to what is happening on the surface. Be sure an area of emphasis is established in each design.

There should be some white or light-value areas near the center of interest, as well as light values that lead the eye from the center of interest to the white corners. If these light values have been lost in the painting process, they can now be reestablished by collaging again. Use a semi-opaque paper (such as Unryu or Yoroshi) and collage pieces where needed. The papers can be toned completely or partially to work into the collaged surface. They should not appear to float above the surface or seem glued on top of the painting. You can recollage several times, until the design is satisfactory. Check the principles of design—balance, movement, emphasis, contrast, unity, pattern—and adjust as needed.

Rotate the finished designs and notice any obvious directional orientations. Most designs made in this way will have several viewing situations that feel comfortable. Remember that the purpose of this exercise is to establish methods of working with the medium; to become aware of some of the possible textural effects; to enjoy the process; and to begin to see how the painting itself can suggest techniques and provide directions.

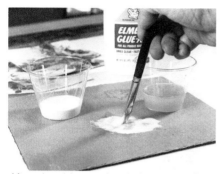

After sketching and painting the surface with initial colors, you are ready to try the basic layering process. Mix glue and water to the consistency of thick cream.

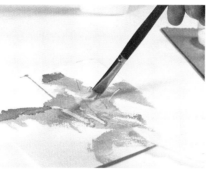

Apply the glue and water mixture to the painted surface in an area a little larger than the size of the torn piece of Oriental paper. Brush firmly, but do not scrub.

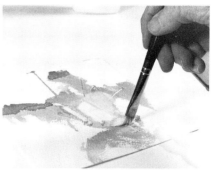

After applying the textured paper, use the same brush—but do not add more glue—to stick the paper firmly in place. Seal all edges to the ground.

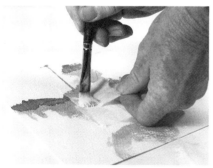

Keep adding pieces of paper until as much of the painted surface is covered as desired.

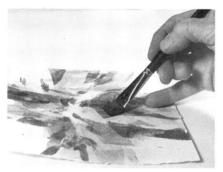

When dry, use a flat watercolor brush to add color. Use a nearly dry brush at first, to remain cognizant of the textures.

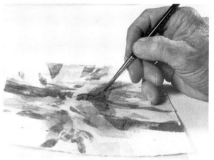

Line can be added with a pointed brush. Use existing textures and shapes to key the placement and direction of line.

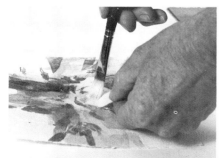

If necessary, parts may be recollaged for example, to reintroduce light values.

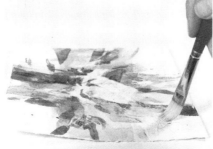

Use fibered papers as transitions to unify the positive and negative areas.

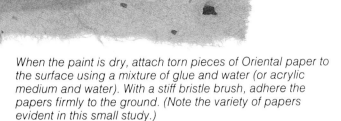

EXPLORING THE
LAYERING PROCESS

Use this demonstration as a guideline. On a 7¹/₂-inch (19 cm) square of 300 lb. Arches rough paper, paint a cruciform design in watercolor. The crossing of vertical and horizontal bridges creates a natural area of emphasis. Spatter and scratch out color to provide an initial indication of texture

When the paint is dry, attach torn pieces of Oriental paper to the surface using a mixture of glue and water (or acrylic medium and water). With a stiff bristle brush, adhere the papers firmly to the ground. (Note the variety of papers evident in this small study.)

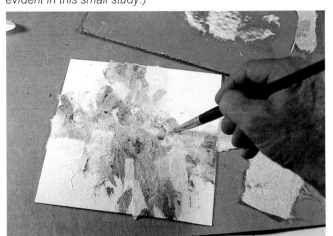

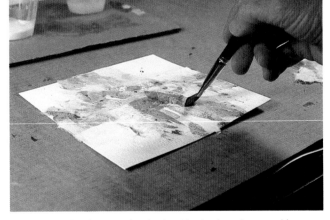

When the glue is completely dry, the textured ground is ready to accept color. Use a fairly dry brush and colors dark enough in value for the textures to be easily seen. Establish color dominance early in the process, but also remember to leave light-value areas to provide passage to the center of interest.

Textures can be enhanced and pattern and visual movement established by adding color washes. Here the layering is evident: you can see initial color showing through the collaged papers, along with added color on top. If you encounter loose (unglued) paper edges while painting, scrape them off with a fingernail, brush handle, or razor blade.

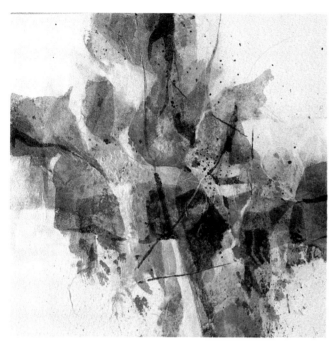

Next, apply darker washes, but preserve the color dominance. As you add color shapes, key them to existing shapes and fibers, following paths, edges, and lines already in existence. Try to distribute color over the surface to establish balance. Be sure to let the color dry somewhat while you're working because very wet papers absorb color too readily. (It's a good idea to work on several paintings at one time.) To bring the painting into focus, concentrate the visual activity near the center of interest. Begin to add dark accents there with both shape and line. Let existing fibers suggest a path for your lines. Also begin to strengthen contrasts—as was done by adding some blues to the warm colors here.

In the final stages you should pull your painting together. Complementary accents, spattering, and colored lines can all help to establish unity. Notice here how cool blues have been pulled over existing warm color shapes and whites to unify the surface. Additional lines help tie the positive and negative areas together. If necessary, you can recollage to emphasize the visual passage of light to the center of interest.

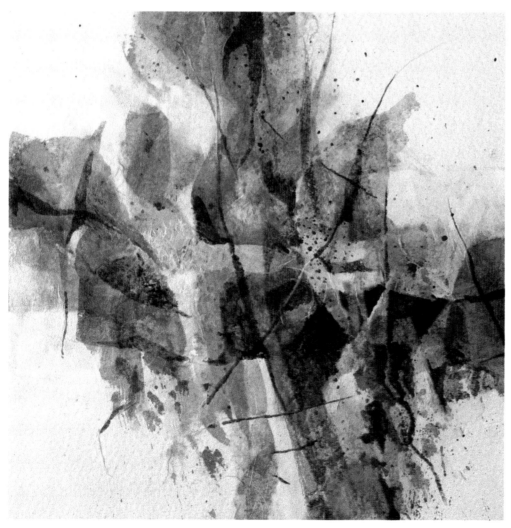

ENRICHING THE SURFACE

FLATTENING AND MATTING THE WORK

By adding watercolor paint to the collaged papers, an infinite variety of textures can be exposed and enhanced. This process is rather passive, however, since the textures emerge almost without effort. You may wish to become more active in adding textures, using a variety of tools and materials.

Pencils, colored pencils, Prismacolors, or pastels can be stroked across the surface, using the point or side. Each leaves a different mark and reacts to the surface in unique ways. The dry collaged surface also accepts pen and ink, fountain pens, and markers. Experiment with thick and thin lines, in black or in color. Follow existing shapes or fibers, or let the line dance freely on the surface.

Try printing on top of the collaged and painted surface to supply further texture or to give texture to flat areas. Use a sponge, crumpled paper, or any other found printing material. You might also print with watercolor on flat papers before collaging them to the surface. Or, when the collaged and painted surface is dry, try sponging off all or part of it. Use a damp sponge (too much water will lift off some of the papers). Wipe firmly and quickly, leaving some of the color in cracks and on some textured surfaces. This technique may work better at one time than another because of differences in the application and amount of glue, types and thicknesses of collaged papers, or absorbency of the surface. Sometimes color will soak in deeply and other times remain on the surface, easy to lift off. Experimentation is essential.

You can also blot with tissue while applying washes over the collaged surface. Or scratch the wash with sticks or the brush handle to move the color around and add texture to some areas of the painting. Because of the variables, no two surfaces will be exactly alike, and you must adapt quickly to what is happening on the paper. This is at once a challenge and a source of surprise and possible exhilaration. Dealing with these unpredictable situations helps you adapt to accidental developments in any kind of painting.

When used alone, watercolors may cause even 300 lb. paper to arch, bow, and wrinkle. These irregularities become even more evident when watercolor and collage are combined. There is a simple way to flatten watercolor and collage works, as well as regular watercolors, prior to matting and framing.

Obtain white blotter sheets, available in several sizes up to 40 × 60 inches (102 × 152 cm) from art supply stores. Cut them 2 inches (5 cm) larger than the paper you wish to flatten. If you do mostly full-sheet paintings, then cut the blotters 24 × 32 inches (61 × 81 cm). You can also flatten two half-sheets or four quarter-sheets in this setup. Now cut two pieces of ½- or ⅝-inch plywood the same size—or use several old drawing boards.

Turn a painting over, dampen the back side with a moist sponge, and then place it face down on a blotter, with another blotter on top of it. Moisten another painting and place it face down on top of this pile. Continue until all the paintings are on the stack, each sandwiched between blotters. The paintings should all be the same size—or place two half-sheets side by side to form a full sheet. Now put this entire stack between the two sheets of plywood and either place a heavy weight on top (such as a five-gallon can of rocks) or use four, six, or eight C-clamps to exert pressure. Leave this arrangement for a day or two before removing the flattened sheets, which are ready for matting, trimming, framing, or storage.

Textured surfaces need mats to contain the intense visual activity, whether the work is representational or nonobjective. For the six nonobjective squares you painted, make several mats with dimensions of about 4 × 6 inches (10 × 15 cm) inside and 8 × 10 inches (20 × 25 cm) outside. You can probably purchase die-cut mats about this size from a framing shop or your art supply dealer. Now take one of your nonobjective collages and hold the mat over it in different places. Observe the variety of images available. Turn the painting in

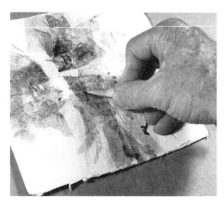

To enhance textures on the collaged surfaces, experiment with pencil.

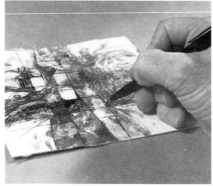

Also explore pen and ink.

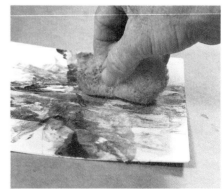

If values become too dark, try lightening areas by lifting some of the color off the surface with a sponge.

20

several directions and again move the mat. Some of these small images may even suggest landscapes, still lifes, or figures. Watch for visual movement, balance, and an area of emphasis (see the examples on this and following pages). When you find a design that feels comfortable and pleases you, tape the mat and collage together. Do this for several small images.

The selection of an area to mat reveals much about your design sense. You may favor images that have a high or a low horizon, fast or slow visual movement, dramatic contrasts or subtle color nuances, a vertical or horizontal orientation. These abstract designs may be finished artworks in their own right, ready for framing or they may serve as concepts or sketches for larger paintings (see pages 42–44). Hang several in your studio; they may suggest possible painting formats as you study them from time to time.

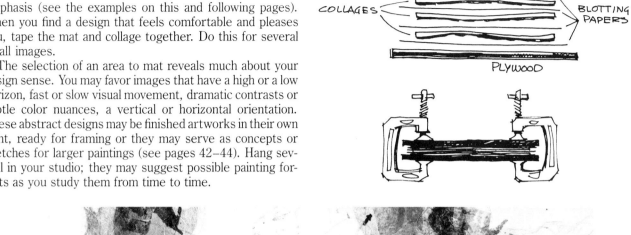

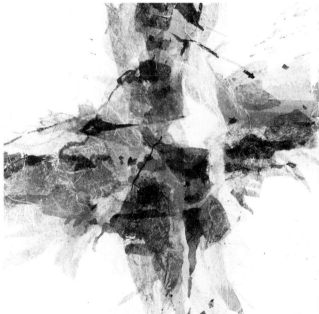

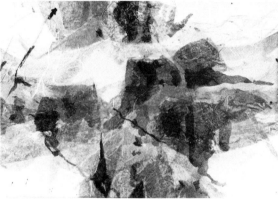

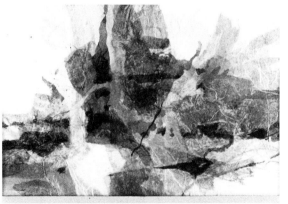

Use a mat with a 4 x 6-inch opening to select several possible subjects for your 7½-inch square painting. The square work above is shown with three of the many possible choices.

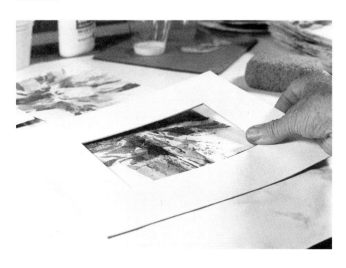

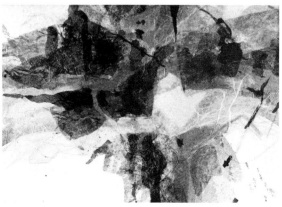

THE IMPORTANCE OF PERSONAL CHOICE

When selecting a composition, bear in mind that there is no absolute and best choice. Instead, there are usually several good selections. Find the one that appeals to you personally.

The examples shown here are some of the possible design motifs from the demonstration on pages 18–19. Different artists would undoubtedly select different designs because their tastes would differ. You may wish to make a small paper mat, or take two small L-shaped pieces of paper, and see how many other compositions you are able to find in the finished demonstration.

Mat sizes for your work may also vary as you choose. Sometimes the entire work can be matted as it stands. That is another choice for you to make.

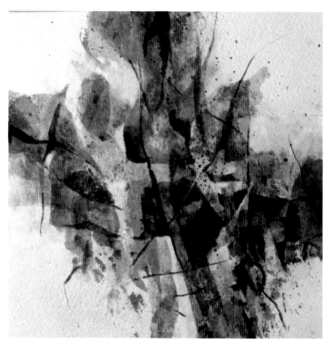

The six designs have been selected from the finished demonstration painting shown at right, but it is possible to find many more. If you make a paper mat with an opening about the same size as these examples and move it around, you can select additional designs on your own.

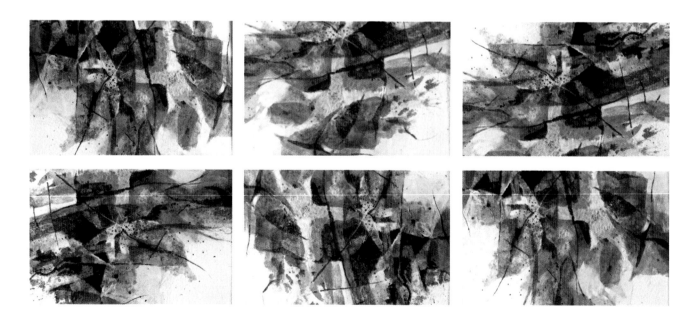

ANOTHER PROJECT

If you were intrigued with the 7½-inch squares, try the same technique on a larger scale. Cut two 15 × 15-inch (38 × 38 cm) squares from a full sheet of 300 lb. paper or from watercolor board. Using the bridging concept, select a center of interest and begin to apply watercolor to bridge the space, both vertically and horizontally. Use a limited palette and apply the color quickly. Spatter, blot, and scratch out as you feel the need.

When the sheets are dry, collage as before, using larger pieces of torn or cut paper. Torn pieces will create an organic surface, while cut pieces will generate a geometric feeling. Then, when the collaged surface is dry, begin exploring the textures with watercolor washes. Be sure to work to the edges of the sheet. Concentrate on the abstract qualities of shape, line, color, value, and texture and how to distribute them on the sheet. After you have worked for a while, look at the evolving image to see if it suggests some representational subject. Turn the sheet to examine several angles. If no possibilities exist, paint a bit more and stop for further evaluation.

It is possible that no representational forms will emerge, and the design can be completed as a nonobjective work, just as you finished the smaller studies. If some recognizable images are suggested, however, begin to develop them into definite representational objects. Trees, rocks, streams, coasts, flowers, still life objects, and people may be drawn from the textures, colors, and values. Often subjects used in recent paintings are the first to emerge.

Draw outlines with pencil or brush if desired, or define forms with shapes and washes. You can develop the entire surface into a representational statement, or leave parts as semi-abstract environments for several clearly defined forms. Exercise your imagination. All parts of the painting must work together, but they need not look exactly alike or be carried to the same degree of completeness.

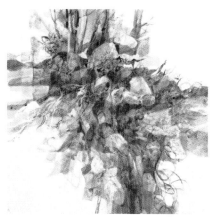

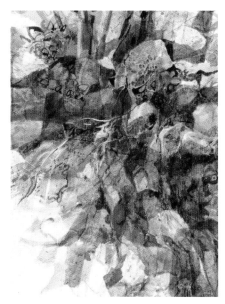

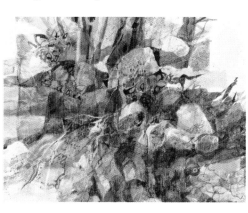

The two 15-inch-square (38 cm) paintings were developed from abstract, cruciform designs. The nonobjective collaged surfaces began to suggest representational subjects: a rocky, autumn hillside and a vase of flowers. The pieces were then handled as representational paintings, but the integrity of the collage process was retained. Again, you can use rectangular mats to choose a variety of smaller designs for each square painting.

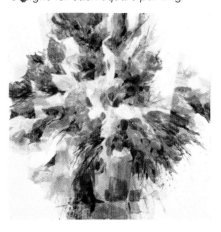

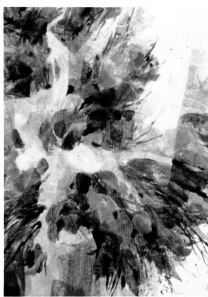

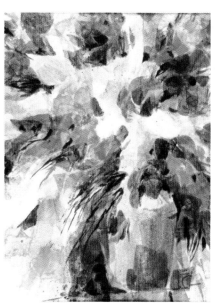

23

COLOR AND STONE/CATHEDRAL
IMPRESSION. Watercolor, 22" × 30"
(56 × 76 cm). Collection of Michael
David Birns.

In this watercolor, you can see the same
compositional elements as in the
collage below: bridging, extension to
the borders of the sheet, light values
leading to the area of emphasis, strong
value contrasts, and transitional
passages from negative to positive
areas. Much of what has been said, in
connection with collage techniques,
about design concepts and the
construction of paintings is directly
applicable to making paintings in any
medium, including watercolor.

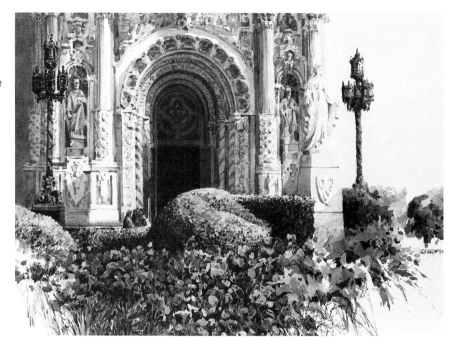

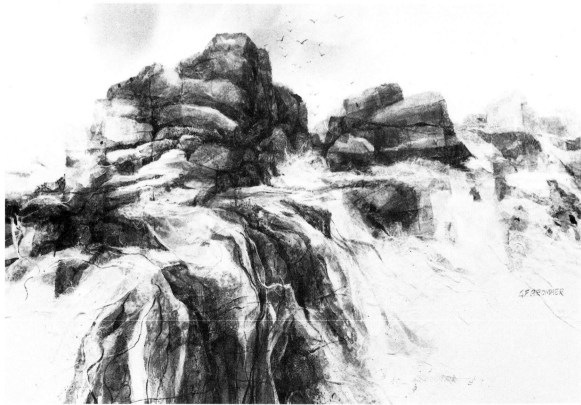

SURF AND ROCKS. Watercolor and collage, 15" × 22" (38 × 56 cm). Private
collection.

Although this painting was begun on a rectangular rather than a square surface, it
was developed from an abstract bridging concept similar to that used in the
demonstration on pages 18–19. After the cruciform design was painted in
abstract shapes, it was collaged with Oriental papers, with no definite subject in
mind. Only then did the subject of coastal rocks and surf suggest itself and
receive its final articulation.

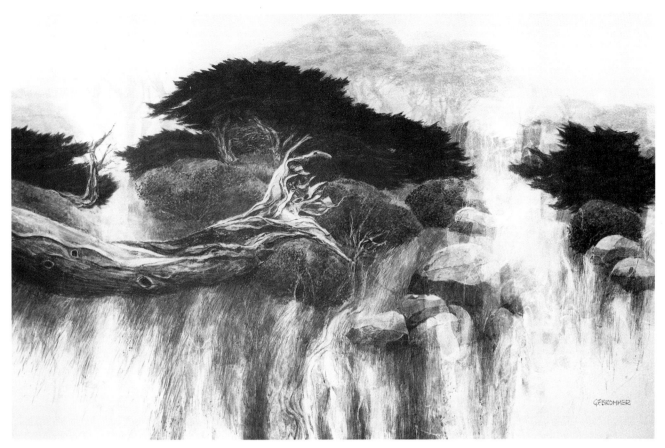

FOGGY CARMEL MORNING. Watercolor and collage on watercolor board, 24" × 36" (61 × 91 cm). Collection of Mickie Moore.

Look at the accompanying sketch to see the basic cruciform design, with its powerful horizontal and vertical bridging. Then notice in the final painting how the passage of light values from negative space to the center of interest (the tree root and dark cypress tree) reinforces the bridging concept. To develop the painting, I first laid in large color shapes to generally locate many of the landscape elements and then applied Oriental papers to create a foggy atmosphere. By painting the background trees in middle values and later covering them with lacy papers, I enhanced the foggy mood. Varied papers also help to articulate the textures of faceted rocks, stringy grass, gnarled tree trunks, and bushy shrubs.

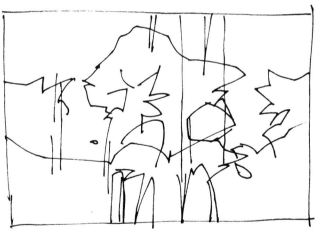

2 EXPERIMENTING WITH WHITES

One of the most controversial aspects of watercolor painting is the handling of white space. Some artists demand that white be present in all watercolors, while others demand just as vehemently that white appear in paintings only if it can be seen in the subject. These extreme views can be confusing to artists just beginning to explore the joys and complexities of watercolor. It is certainly true that superb watercolors have been painted both with and without white spaces.

The essential point to understand here is the necessity for value control and contrast in all types of painting. Painting relies on the difference between light and dark values to articulate its message. All the principles of design—emphasis, balance, contrast, pattern, movement, rhythm, and unity—can be defined and described in terms of dark and light values. Black-and-white photographs of paintings, which rely on value contrast, can be used to study and understand these design principles.

In traditional transparent watercolor painting, opaque whites are excluded from the artist's palette. For pristine whites to be included in a painting, the paper must remain uncolored—untouched by pigment at all. This can be accomplished simply by "saving" the white areas and not painting certain predetermined spaces on the surface. Whites can also be saved by blocking out some parts of the surface with a masking fluid such as Miskit or Maskoid. The masking fluid resists the application of watercolor; when it is later removed, the white of the paper remains. These white areas may then need to be integrated into the surrounding color areas with transitional tones.

Both of these processes require advance planning, as the location of white areas must be predetermined. Although whites or light values can be moved or added by sponging the color and lifting it off the surface, this method is usually only partially successful. With collage techniques, however, whites or light values can be introduced (or reintroduced) at any convenient time. Indeed, experimenting with the use of opaque white paint and/or collaged papers can increase your understanding of the importance of light values in painting. It then becomes easier to plan ahead and save whites in traditional watercolor painting techniques.

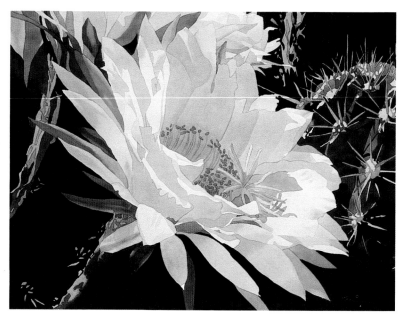

CACTUS FLOWER, by Virginia Pochmann. Watercolor, 20″ × 28″ (51 × 71 cm). Courtesy of the artist.

Virginia Pochmann's flower paintings are dramatic and vital. Working from her own photographs, which she carefully composes, she masks out the positive spaces and paints freely in the background areas, often working in abstract patterns. After these negative spaces are filled and the masking fluid is removed, the flowers are confidently painted to reveal structure and substance. Note the wide range of warm grays in the flower petals and the passage in middle values from the flower to the background.

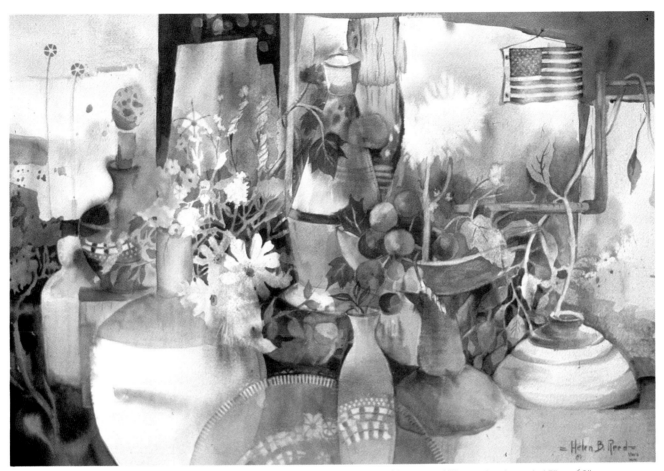

RED, WHITE AND BLUE STILL LIFE, by Helen B. Reed. Watercolor on cold-pressed illustration board, 15" × 22" (38 × 56 cm). Collection of the artist.

Helen Reed began this painting by brushing large, middle-value washes in abstract patterns. In one area, she dropped salt to create textural contrast. When the surface was dry, Reed used paper stencils and a flat, 3/4-inch white synthetic brush to lift off color and introduce light values in the painting. After establishing the light pattern, she worked in dark, negative areas to strengthen the value contrasts and design. The objects in the still life are imaginary; they developed as Reed reacted to the shapes resulting from the lifting process.

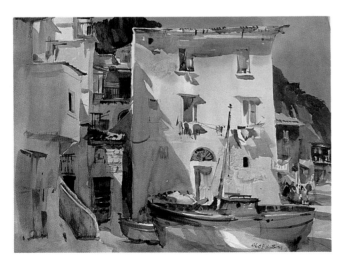

SORRENTO—MARINA GRANDE, by Robert E. Wood. Watercolor, 22" × 30" (56 × 76 cm). Collection of Mr. and Mrs. Roger Canter.

Robert E. Wood painted this watercolor on location in Italy. He sketched the subject quickly and saved the white spaces by painting around them. When the major shapes had been established and middle and dark values painted in, he tied the white spaces to the rest of the painting with transitional washes, providing passages to other light- and middle-value areas. Careful observation and complete control of the painting process are needed to work in this direct way.

OPAQUE LAYERING

Whites can be brought back into watercolor paintings through a variety of techniques. Some artists view these techniques as defensive, as efforts to save watercolors that are not developing successfully. But these processes can also be considered offensive, and they can become tools for creating effective visual statements.

Whites may be brought back into water-media paintings by using opaque media, such as white gesso (Permanent Pigments makes a powder: Gesso Ground Dry Mixture), white casein, white gouache (designers colors), or thinned acrylic gesso. Opaque whites are usually applied with a bristle brush, which lends a textural, painterly quality to the surface. These whites can then be left alone (to remain white), given washes of watercolor, or worked over with traditional watercolor techniques.

Another way to bring white shapes or areas back into the composition is to collage white paper onto the painted surfaces. You can use small pieces of 140 lb. or 300 lb. watercolor paper or larger chunks—even half-sheets or more. Full-strength white glue or Yes! glue will adhere these heavy papers to the painted surface. You may also use opaque Oriental papers for the same purpose, or try a number of other boards and papers. Papers that will lie flat when collaged are best. Experiment with different Oriental papers. Many are not opaque enough to block out pre-painted colors, but some are. Also try overlapping and layering several papers to create opaque white passages.

To lighten a value, rather than create a pure white shape, you can apply white ink or thinned white gesso, casein, or gouache as a veil over a color area. Thin Oriental papers can also be used to lighten existing values.

Explore various combinations of these opaque layering techniques to create areas that are both white and textured. You can plan the white areas in your original painting concept, or introduce them later, as the painting surface is developed. Depending on the needs of the painting, you can let these areas stand as opaque white passages or tone them and work them back into the surface of the painting.

Working with opaque whites in this way can help you comprehend the importance of light values in developing visual movement, contrast, and emphasis in watercolor paintings. Once these concepts are firmly grasped, they become part of your visual vocabulary, available for use in any kind of painting.

STONEHENGE. Watercolor, gesso, casein, collage, and ink, 22" × 30" (56 × 76 cm). Collection of Mr. and Mrs. Robert A. Kellen.

The whites in this painting are a combination of Oriental papers, glazes of diluted white gesso, and opaque white casein. Some whites have been brushed on in diluted glazes; others, printed with the edge of a piece of cardboard. Notice that the whites occur in both positive and negative spaces and link the foreground, middle ground, and background. The cubistic feeling also adds unity by involving the negative spaces in the texture and solidity of the gigantic stone columns. The emphasis on verticality, within the horizontal format, suggests a spiritual mood.

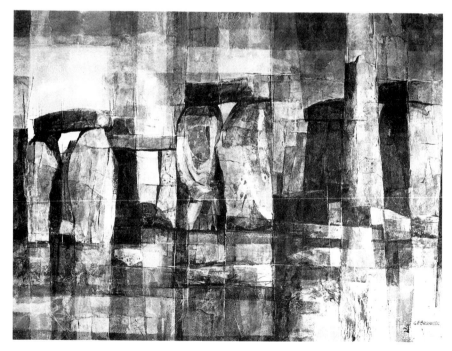

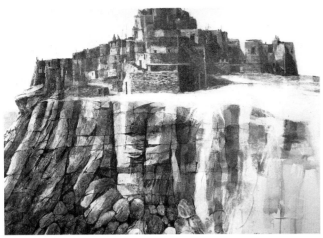

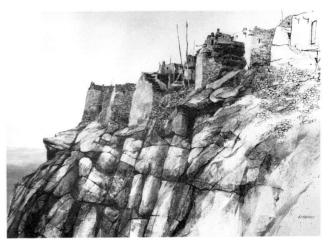

HOPI CITADEL. Watercolor and collage, 22" × 30" (56 × 76 cm). Collection of Fireside Gallery, Carmel, California.

Here white Oriental papers, adhered over the collaged and painted surface, tie positive and negative spaces together, provide visual movement to the area of emphasis, and strengthen the white shapes and thus the dramatic contrast in the painting. Most of these final paper additions have been left untouched because a hint of color shows through the paper layering. This provides enough tone to unify the whites with the rest of the painting, so they do not appear to be afterthoughts, foreign to the surface.

EDGE OF THE MESA. Watercolor, collage, and ink, 22" × 30" (56 × 76 cm). Private collection.

The heavy, opaque papers added to this surface create impressive textured areas, much like the rocky ledges on which the pueblo is located. I glued 300 lb. rough and 140 lb. cold-pressed watercolor paper in several places on the painted surface and then collaged Oriental papers over much of the surface to unify the textures. The drawing in the upper right, done with a stick and India ink on top of collaged watercolor papers, leads directly into the painted sections.

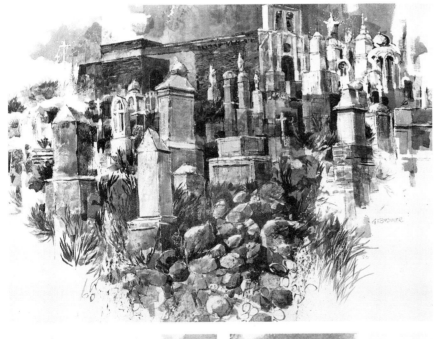

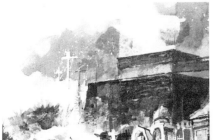

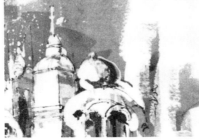

OQUITOA. Watercolor, gesso, and ink, 22" × 30" (56 × 76 cm). Collection of the artist.

After sketching the old Mexican mission and its surrounding monuments and painting them in watercolor, I used gesso to structure a white pattern throughout the work. Then I added lines with a stick and India ink, and applied watercolor over many of the gessoed areas, to work them back into the painting surface. Some white, gessoed areas remain untouched, however; they provide passage from the negative spaces to the subject's central core and also describe the whitewashed surfaces of some of the monuments. They are not just "leftover" whites, but strong, essential, planned parts of the painting.

DIRECTING VISUAL MOVEMENT

Visual movement directs the viewer's eye on a path through the work, usually from the bottom edge (and other edges, to a lesser degree) to the center of interest. This path can follow a direct, circuitous, zigzag, or S-shaped route. But, regardless of the plan, visual movement is essential in involving all parts of the surface in the composition and creating a coherent statement.

Although visual movement can be established through related lines or shapes, color transitions (cool to warm, for example), or gradual progressions of detail or color intensity, it is probably most convincingly plotted and maintained through value contrast. Our eyes move freely and easily over passages of light and dark values that tie parts of paintings together. If passages from one part of the painting to another do not exist, we find ourselves locked in corners and boxes, unable to move comfortably. There should be ways for our eyes to move from the foreground to the background, from the sky to a mountain, from left to right, from trees to a house. Since our eyes move most easily over paths of similar values, it is important that you learn to control and direct these passages to advantage.

Collage can help you establish visual movement in your paintings. When you apply Oriental papers to the surface, you become more aware of the importance of light-value areas in creating paths of movement. And if light-value pathways are lost in the painting process, they can be reintroduced by collaging white papers in appropriate places.

You should begin to sense movement in your work from the first preparatory sketches you make. Make thumbnail sketches with linear guidelines or do small value studies that suggest movement. Then, as you make your preliminary marks on the watercolor paper, try to indicate the passages of light and dark that lead to the center of interest. You can use light lines as guides. Some artists tone the entire sheet *except* for a pattern of white, to establish visual movement and a center of interest. If you use collage, you can reinforce your original plan for visual movement as you add the papers. If your plan is somehow obliterated, more papers can be added to reestablish continuity and movement.

Bear in mind that visual movement is almost unrelenting on actual paths, such as a stream, road, trail, or sunlight in a landscape. Often this movement is so strong that it must be slowed in some way to allow the viewer to absorb more from the painting. As the artist, you can establish your own visual movement in the painting—movement that need not follow natural paths. This movement is usually controlled by using similar light and dark values, even though it may skip across dissimilar objects, colors, and surfaces. In a still life, for example, a light-value path might skip from a vase to flowers to a cloth to an apple. Collaging with light values can help you understand and use this kind of movement, and help you see the larger, light-value shapes and areas rather than the objects in your painting.

Because our eyes also move along dark-value passages, these too must be controlled. If you concentrate on light-value movement, however, the darks will probably take care of themselves. If darks become isolated in a painting, it is easier to adjust and tie them together than to make major adjustments in a confusing light pattern.

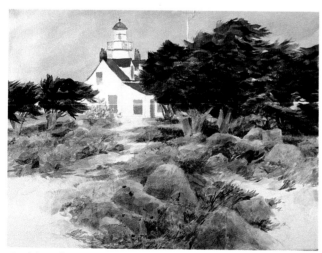

As this collage develops, it becomes obvious that the foreground is monotonous, that the upright rock is not in keeping with the overall design, and that passage from the lower right corner (negative space) to the center of interest has been cut off.

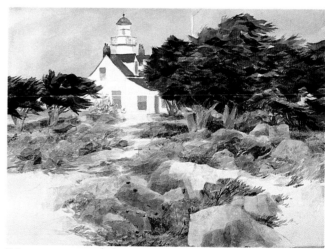

When opaque and medium-weight Oriental papers are collaged in selected areas, they appear white. Notice the change in rock sizes and shapes, as well as the opening up of a light passage to the center of interest.

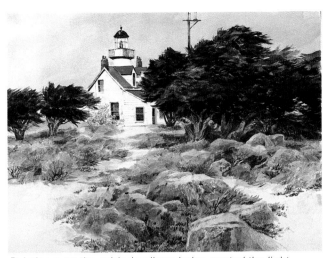

Painting over the added collage helps control the light passage and ties the rocks' character to the rest of the painting.

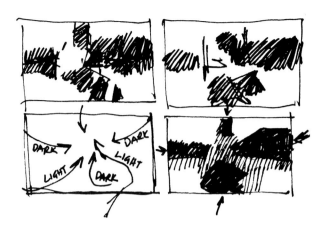

These sketches show some of the thinking involved in determining the visual movement in this painting.

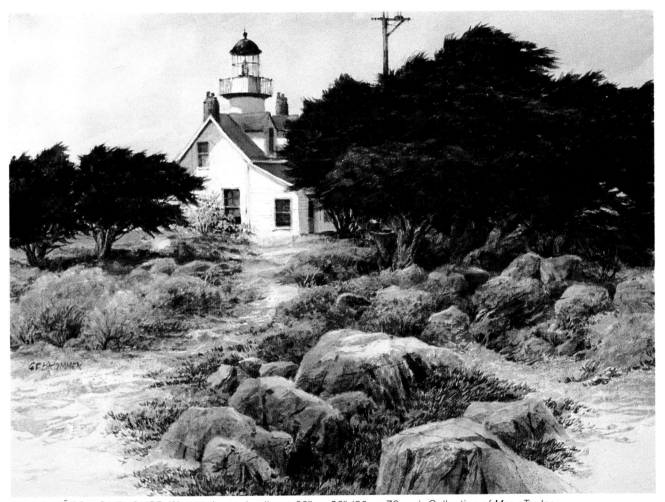

POINT PIÑOS LIGHTHOUSE. Watercolor and collage, 22″ × 30″ (56 × 76 cm). Collection of Mary Taylor.

Final colors, textures, and unifying shadows are put in. Notice that the light now moves from the sand to the rocks to the bushes to the path to the lighthouse as it travels from the lower right corner. The impelling natural path to the lighthouse has been disrupted in places to slow the visual movement.

DESIGNING WITH VALUE CONTRASTS

Expertise in working with value contrasts will enable you to compose paintings more confidently. Working with collage can help you to understand the appropriate use of whites in designing space, because areas can be worked and reworked until they are successful. This knowledge can be readily translated into any medium.

Study the illustrations on this page to see how valuable the use of black and white can be in establishing pictorial formats and then experiment on your own. Take pieces of black construction paper and arrange them several times on a white background. Placing a mat over each arrangement helps to identify the picture plane and confine the visual activity. Now glue some black construction-paper shapes to a white board and add torn pieces of Oriental paper. This will produce textures and a variety of gray shapes, which may suggest concepts for full-scale paintings.

Next, use dark-value magazine pages instead of black construction paper, and tear and position the pieces as in the examples on the facing page. Textures and grays, as well as color, may already be indicated. Watercolor or acrylic washes can be used in the white spaces to provide transitional values between whites and darks.

Experiment with a wide variety of materials to clinch the visual movement in your painting. Be sensitive to the "feel" of these experimental pieces, and try to adapt all that you have learned so far. Try, for instance, combining these black-and-white studies with the idea of the square abstractions on pages 18–19. Push yourself to explore other ways of using value contrasts, textures, and white spaces in your paintings. All artists, regardless of their preferred medium, can benefit from a few hours of work with these collage studies.

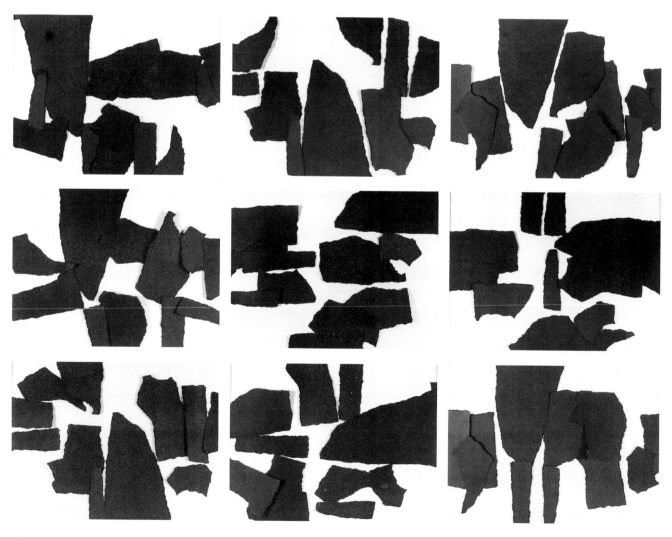

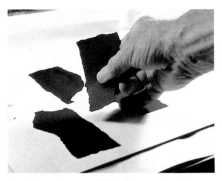

Position pieces of black construction paper on a sheet of white illustration board. Try several configurations, then glue one arrangement in place.

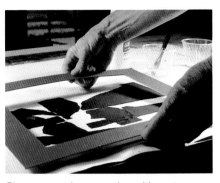

Place a mat in several positions to see which composition seems to have the most potential for development.

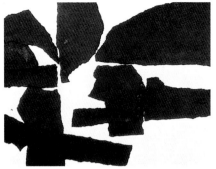

Select one design and mark it on the surface.

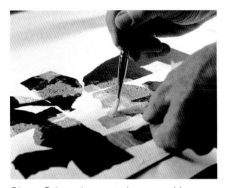

Place Oriental papers in several locations and collage them in place as transitions and continuations of existing contours.

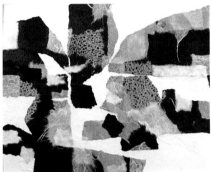

Add some black papers for emphasis and design interest. Check for movement, passage, pattern, and center of interest.

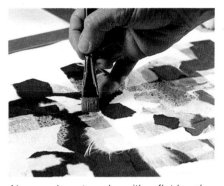

Now apply watercolor with a flat brush to selected areas to emphasize texture, passage, and overall compositional unity.

The finished collage may suggest a variety of possible paintings; it also illustrates the satisfying results of designing with simple elements.

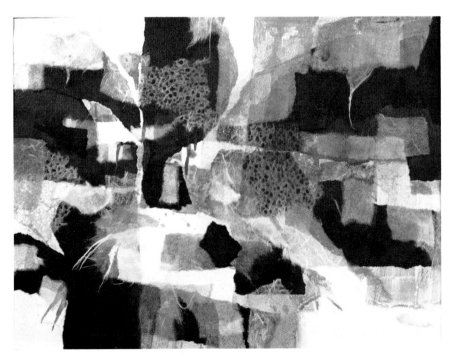

3
GENERATING DYNAMIC COMPOSITIONS

In painting, composition and design refer to the satisfying arrangement of forms, colors, shapes, and values on the picture plane. Often it is easier to define these terms than it is to make them work in a painting. Entire books have been written to help artists understand and use design intelligently (see the bibliography).

Although there are no rigid rules for composition, there are some principles that can help painters organize the spaces in their work. But keep in mind that design is an aspect of art, not a science. All design principles are simply guidelines; they are not meant to stand in the way of creative expression. Design principles are the grammar of visual communication; they tell us how we can use our visual vocabulary in the most effective ways.

From the beginning concept to the final touches, the development of your painting involves design—where to place the dominant shapes, where to locate the center of interest, which values to use, how to relate colors, where to develop visual movement, and on and on. Much of what you do is intuitive and is governed by all the visual experiences you have had in your life. But painting also involves many decisions, many choices, many options for the artist. How you respond to these options reveals your personal sense of design.

Design consists of understanding visual relationships and effectively using balance, pattern, rhythm, movement, proportion, contrast, and emphasis. All these principles should be considered, but the overriding principles are unity and variety. Unity refers to oneness, to the comfortable sensation that everything in the painting works together. At the same time variety is essential to avoid monotony and make a painting visually exciting.

THE DESIGN PROCESS

Your first major decision in making a painting is to choose the size, shape, and proportions that will work best with your subject. Should the painting be horizontal, vertical, or square? Large or small? How wide or how high?

Once the shape of the painting is determined, you must locate the center of interest, where the movement generated in the painting will come to a culmination. Euclid, a sage of ancient Greece, proposed the golden mean as the perfect proportional placement for the elements in a painting. His subdivisions of space were based on exact measurements, but a generalization of this arrangement can be made by placing a tic-tac-toe configuration inside your established borders (see the diagram). The four places where these lines intersect are preferred places for centers of interest. Notice that this rule of thumb eliminates clumsy locations such as the corners or dead-center. Although excellent paintings can be made with the center of interest at one of these problematic locations, they should generally be avoided.

A few basic design formats are sketched here to acquaint you with some compositional possibilities. They may appear simplistic, but they are based on observations of nature and provide a basic means of visual organization. Most paintings fit into one or a combination of these basic configurations. Again, however, there are no absolute rules. Successful paintings have been made that ignore any formal directional orientation at all and emphasize overall patterns.

Make your own thumbnail sketches to simplify pictorial material into basic design formats: vertical, horizontal, cruciform (cross-shaped), diagonal, central, or combinations of these. The sketches should help you determine the underlying structure. Remember, however, that these are only guidelines and that there are numerous variations.

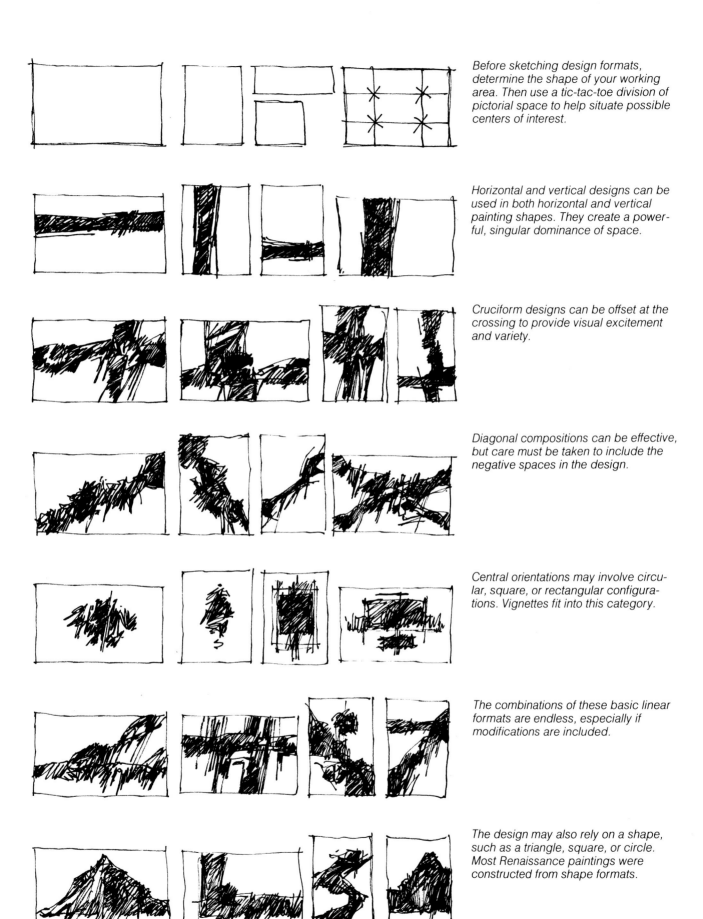

Before sketching design formats, determine the shape of your working area. Then use a tic-tac-toe division of pictorial space to help situate possible centers of interest.

Horizontal and vertical designs can be used in both horizontal and vertical painting shapes. They create a powerful, singular dominance of space.

Cruciform designs can be offset at the crossing to provide visual excitement and variety.

Diagonal compositions can be effective, but care must be taken to include the negative spaces in the design.

Central orientations may involve circular, square, or rectangular configurations. Vignettes fit into this category.

The combinations of these basic linear formats are endless, especially if modifications are included.

The design may also rely on a shape, such as a triangle, square, or circle. Most Renaissance paintings were constructed from shape formats.

DYNAMIC SPATIAL ORGANIZATION

Dynamic organizational concepts can breathe life into paintings and help you say something dramatic about your subject. Essentially, these concepts are ways of organizing the painting space to create an exciting visual statement. Everything in the painting may accentuate an explosive thrust, or the subject may be presented from a worm's-eye view. The possibilities are endless. Developed over many years, these plans become a major part of an artist's style. A study of the prize-winning paintings in national watercolor shows will reveal a variety of choices for dynamic spatial organization.

A good way to become familiar with organizational concepts is to make a series of small watercolor studies that emphasize only the major shapes and movement in paintings. Collage can be added to some or all of your studies to help you emphasize the organizing principles. Use the small studies shown here as a starting point. Also look at catalogs of major shows and art history books. You may wish to keep a notebook with dozens of these ideas and use them in designing your own paintings.

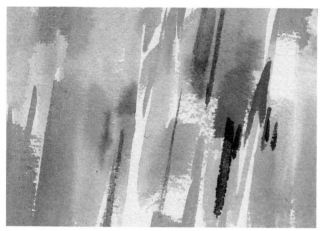

DIRECTIONAL BRUSHSTROKES. When all the brushstrokes are laid down in the same direction, flatness is emphasized and form is minimized. If naturalistic subjects are treated this way, an exciting tension between reality and abstraction will exist. Seurat's dots and Cézanne's squarish strokes create a similar tension, flattening their three-dimensional subject.

TILTING THE FOREGROUND. Instead of using a gradual transition into deep space, you can tilt the foreground, moving everything forward and condensing actual space. Things at your feet are seen vertically while distant objects are seen horizontally.

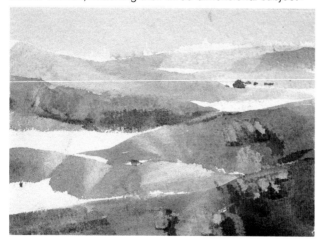

WEDGING. When large shapes are wedged together, our eyes move gradually into the distance, skating from side to side across the wedges. These wedges, which need not be actual land formations, can be defined by varying values.

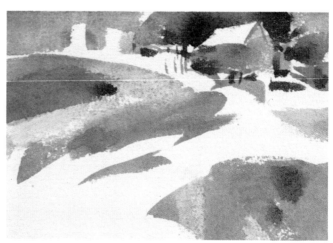

ZIGZAG MOVEMENT. To allow space for a zigzag to develop, you should use a high horizon. Here the movement is defined by the light values, but it could also be articulated by "things" or dark or middle values.

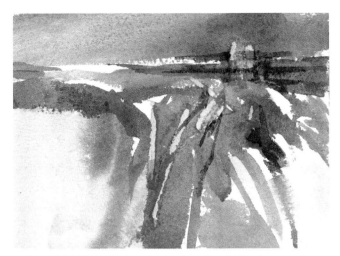

HIGH HORIZON. *Placing the horizon line in the top quarter of the sheet forces movement dramatically upward and visually creates a sense of compression. It allows you to develop the foreground and provides space for establishing visual movement.*

LOW HORIZON. *A low horizon, like a high one, creates an unequal division of space, producing dynamic visual tension. Using a low horizon, you can establish a magnificent sky, with silhouetted forms in the foreground.*

VIGNETTING. *In a complete vignette, the subject is surrounded by white paper, but you can also use partial vignettes at the edges to generate excitement. Keep the corner configurations interesting and different from each other. Provide transitional areas from negative to positive space.*

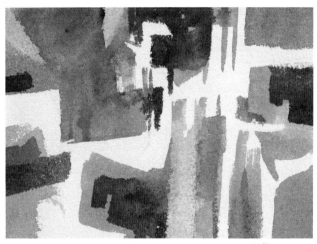

INTERLOCKING SHAPES. *Value contrasts can define interlocking shapes, which fit together, like pieces of a jigsaw puzzle, to unite the surface. Interlocking avoids monotonous shapes and straight edges. This example also shows directional emphasis—in this case, verticality.*

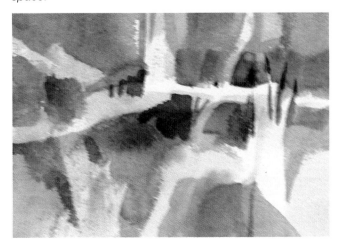

PASSAGE OR LINKAGE. *The emphasis in passage is on connecting similar values. Squint your eyes to see it in this example, where light values are linked together; some darks and middle values are also linked. Subject matter here is lost in favor of pattern.*

WORKING FROM NATURE TO ABSTRACTION

Using collage techniques can help you understand how to design abstract compositions with nature as a starting point. This demonstration shows you how to use the painting itself as resource material, instead of constantly referring back to an original photograph for details and directions. This is an important concept for creative artists to understand and nurture.

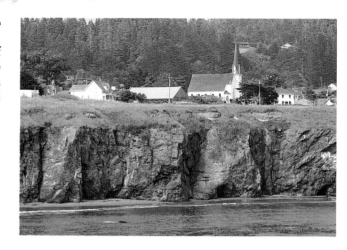

I took this photograph of the California coastal village of Mendocino with the idea of someday using it as the subject for a painting, so the center of interest—the church—is already favorably situated. The format is primarily horizontal, with several vertical thrusts that stabilize the movement.

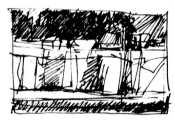 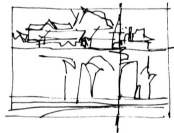 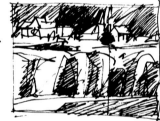

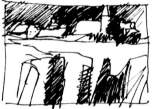 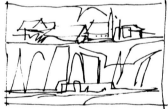 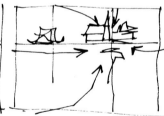

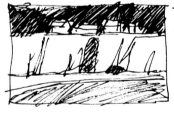 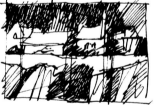

These sketches show several organizational possibilities. Notice how basic visual movement and compositional balance are explored.

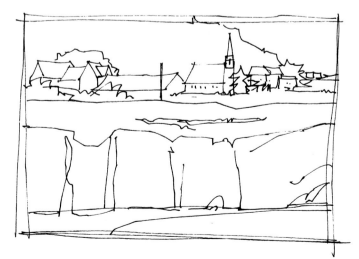

After exploring different design formats, I make a simple drawing to indicate the arrangement of the major shapes in the scene—cliff, beach and water, buildings and trees, background. This drawing is based on my sketches rather than on the photograph; in turn, the drawing becomes the basis for my initial painting.

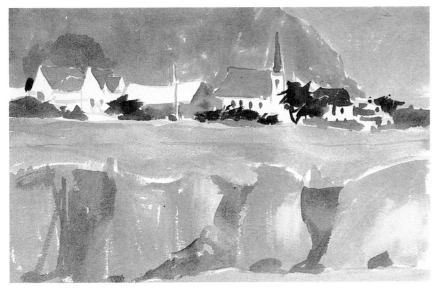

With a large round brush, I outline the major shapes on a quarter-sheet (11 × 15 inches [28 × 38 cm]) of Arches 300 lb. rough paper. Knowing that this image will be drastically altered, I don't take special care to make anything precise—this is just a nice, loose statement. The colors approximate the light values of local colors in the photograph, but all the landscape elements are reduced to simple, basic shapes.

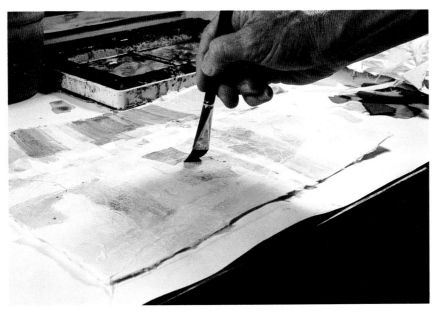

When collaging the first pieces of Oriental paper to the painting, I allow abstract shapes to dominate. Instead of tearing the papers into specific shapes to cover hills, houses, or cliffs, I use them as they come and let them overlap painted shapes. New, collaged shapes begin to emerge, developing rhythm and pattern.

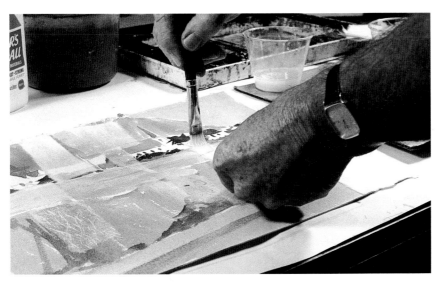

The original subject is neglected as different Oriental papers are stuck down in vertical and horizontal orientations. Some of these papers obliterate color, while others allow color to show through. Note how the texture of some papers is enhanced by color showing through. Already, the surface has an abstract quality not present in the simple painting. Now I begin to apply paint to the textured ground.

At this point a decision must be made. Should the painting follow its current abstract direction? Or should the original scene be reconstructed on the textured ground? Here I decide to explore the abstract possibilities. Using a relatively dry flat brush, I put down light-value shapes, keyed to existing edges and paper shapes. I am not concerned with the subject matter at this time, only the development of a pleasing abstract design. Although I choose bluish greens and brownish yellows—two dominant hues in the subject—completely different colors could have been selected. The light pattern is beginning to evolve.

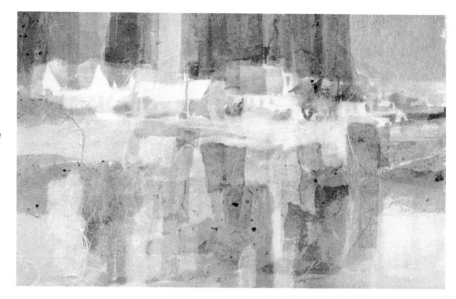

Still using a dry brush, I add darker values, especially in the foreground and the right and left margins, to tie these extremities to the center of interest. The whites remain as part of the established pattern, but the purplish roofs introduce a new color, which must be distributed to several parts of the painting. Notice that I have eliminated the water at the bottom in favor of emphasis on the vertical shafts. The presence of water is implied, however, at the lower left. By bringing out some diagonals, keyed to existing fibers in the papers, I increase the visual interest and counterbalance the emerging strength of the verticals.

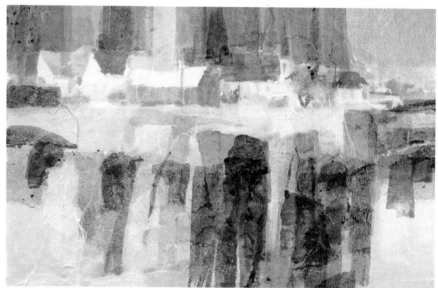

Now I add very dark marks to establish accents and spatter some color for a transition from the white negative space to the textured and painted areas. By strengthening certain colors and introducing grays, I clarify the light pattern and the center of interest. Notice the blues I have added to the lower left to suggest water, and how these blues are repeated in several places on the surface. You should always be aware of size variations in shapes over the surface.

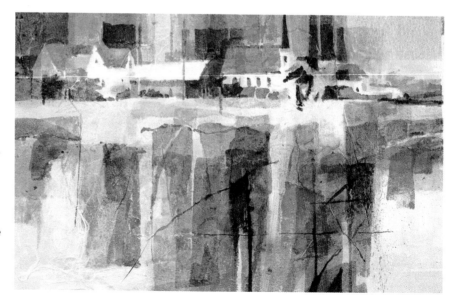

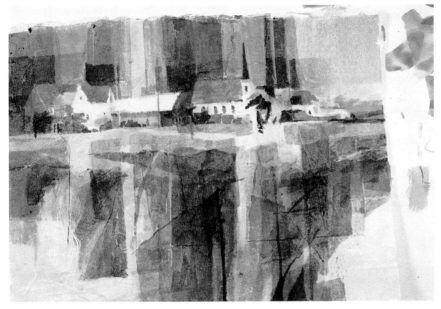

Although I refer to the original photograph for some details, my main interest is still the abstract design. By adding golden yellows and greens to existing shapes and over some whites, I strengthen the presence of the two hues. I also pull greenish blue washes over areas to augment the passage of light. Note the passage from the buildings to the foreground and the background, in both light and middle values. Also observe how diagonals are emphasized in the cliffs to counter overly strong verticals.

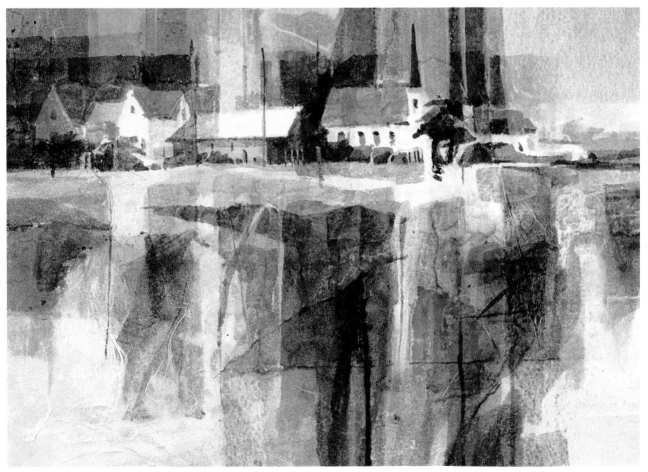

Near the end, I reintroduce collage in several places (lower right, lower center, and upper center) to stress the passage of light. These newly textured areas have to be toned a bit to work them into the surface and establish unity. Finally, using a wet bristle brush and a tissue to lift the paint, I soften a few edges. The result is an abstracted landscape, based on a photograph of nature. The painting could have moved toward a more nonobjective solution at several steps, or it could have moved toward a more naturalistic finish.

WORKING FROM ABSTRACTION TO REPRESENTATION

This demonstration shows you how to make a representational work based on an abstract sketch. The process involves using elements in an abstract design to pull representational subject matter into focus. Existing shapes, textures, and lines become starting points for developing objects. The painting grows organically and you must use imagination to work "inside out"—drawing sustenance from the work itself. So many personal choices are involved as the process unfolds that if a hundred artists worked from the same study, each would end with a different painting.

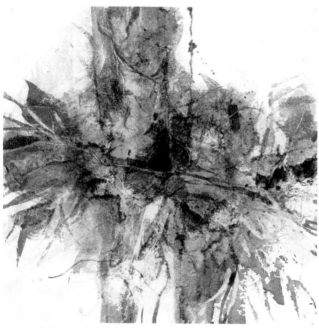

Use a 7¹/₂-inch (19 cm) square abstract collage, prepared as described on pages 18–19, as the starting point for this exercise.

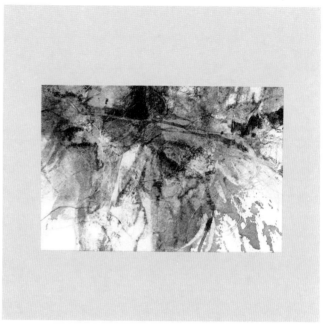

With a 4 × 6-inch (10 × 15 cm) mat, isolate one of the many possible designs in the square. This detail will serve as your "sketch" for the initial development of the painting.

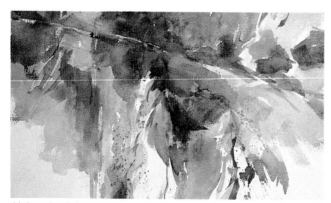

Using the "sketch" as a reference, apply watercolor to a half-sheet of Arches 300 lb. paper. Don't try to copy the sketch exactly; just put in the general colors, shapes, and textures. Detail isn't necessary because the surface will eventually be covered with collage. Now set the painting aside to dry.

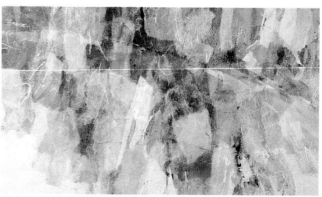

Select about ten different kinds of Oriental paper. Tear and glue them to the painted surface. Again, use the small collage sketch as a general reference for the textures. Overlap and layer the papers to produce a complex ground and then allow the collage to dry completely. Here the entire surface has been covered except for the lower-corner areas; transition fibers tie these areas into the positive shapes.

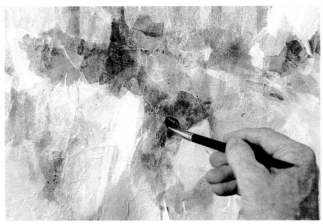

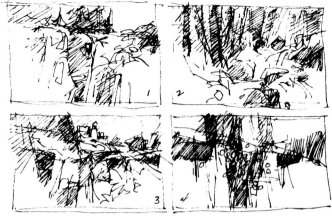

With a relatively dry brush and using the small, matted collage as a guide, begin to define colors and values on the collaged ground. Pause and squint at the unfinished painting. Then add more paint where needed, and look again. Turn the painting and continue evaluating. Here the high horizon of the original sketch seems to provide the best design orientation. Notice that this painting is beginning to suggest a landscape with a cliff in the foreground.

Make some thumbnail sketches to explore the representational possibilities. Shift your focus to see if other images emerge. After defining the cliff with its high horizon (sketch 1), I focused on the top of the painting, which suggested rocks at the base of a waterfall (sketch 2). Looking at the right side of the painting suggested a stormy surf with a lighthouse (sketch 3). I also did a simple abstract pattern (sketch 4).

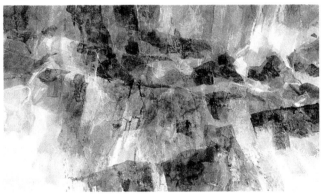

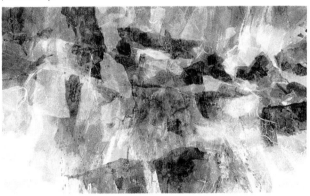

Now put the small collage study aside and develop one of the representational themes. Here I have decided on the stormy surf and lighthouse. I use a flat brush to block in large shapes and pull major parts of the painting into focus. The directional orientation is switched from vertical to horizontal. Fibers and textural shapes suggest rock forms.

Remember that collaged papers can serve as semi-opaque whites in your palette. Here I use white Oriental papers to enlarge the sky shape and clarify the light pattern. The surface now takes on a painterly quality and the final direction of the work is strongly suggested.

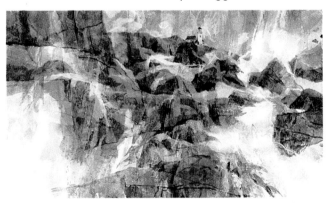

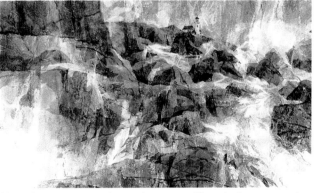

I now use a pointed brush to introduce line and strengthen value contrasts. The lighthouse is finally located and put in place. Because it is in the distance, however, I give it only slight contrast. I want the storm to seem more important than the lighthouse.

Next, I turn my attention to the water. Already there are color and value variations in the whites, due to paint showing through the layers of collaged papers. I now add a little color to the water to introduce texture and provide passage to the rocks. I also pull a few washes over the light areas on the left.

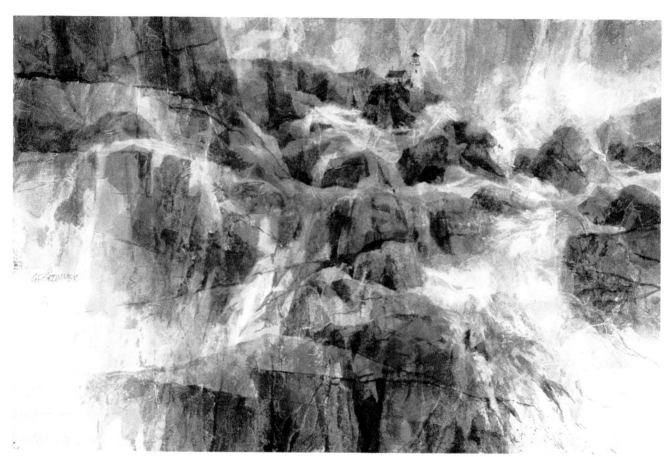

In the final stage, I use a bristle brush and water to soften some edges of color, and then lift them with absorbent tissue. Compare the final painting with the initial collage sketch, and mentally go through the process again. It is exciting to realize that a painting can suggest many different directions as it develops. In the end, the artist makes the choices, based on personal reactions to what is happening in the collage and what seems necessary to make the composition exciting.

These paintings also evolved from small, abstract collages which are shown at the left.

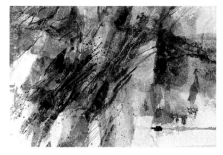

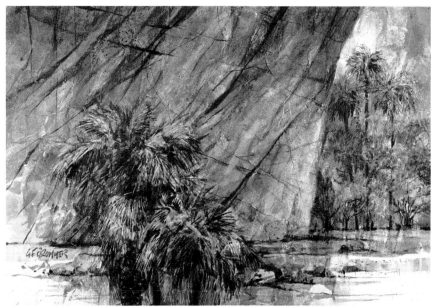

PALM CANYON PALMS. Watercolor and collage, 15" × 22" (38 × 56 cm). Collection of Joy McAllister.

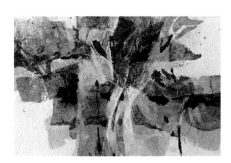

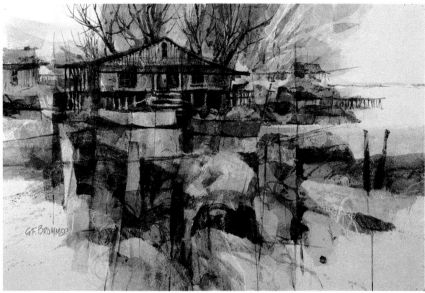

BUCKTOWN, USA. Watercolor and collage, 15" × 22" (38 × 56 cm). Collection of Mr. and Mrs. John Schaeffer.

4
EMPHASIS ON TEXTURE

Texture is a surface quality related to our sense of touch. When an object's surface is verbally described as smooth or sandy or prickly, we develop a concept of the surface qualities, based on our personal experience of actually touching textures.

In a painting, textures can be actual or implied. We can run our fingers over the surface of an acrylic painting, for example, and feel its texture. The surface of watercolor paper may have a texture, referred to as "tooth." These are *actual* textures, which can be experienced through our sense of touch. But you can also create the illusion of texture through visual means.

Watercolor painters work with *implied* textures, visually describing surface qualities that cannot actually be felt by touch. When a tree trunk is painted to look rough and ragged, our eyes interpret the marks and tones, which imply texture. Our minds sense the roughness and comprehend that the tree trunk is rough, even though we cannot actually experience the roughness. A photograph has a similar effect. It makes us visually aware of texture, even though the surface of the photographic paper remains smooth and glossy.

With experimentation, patience, and practice, watercolor painters can simulate almost every existing textural surface. These implied textures are determined by the handling of contrasts in light, shadow, and color. The textural illusions can be so successful that we are tempted to run our fingers over the surface "to make sure" it is really flat.

One strong reason to experiment with collage is that it allows you to experience and work with a variety of actual textures. By combining watercolor with collage, you can make your paintings more compelling in their appeal to viewers' tactile senses. Moreover, using collaged surfaces will make you aware of the possible importance of textures in the construction of successful paintings. You can then transfer that knowledge to the development of direct watercolor paintings.

The examples of actual and implied textures on the facing page should help you sense the importance of texture. Our world would be a peculiar, surreal place if everything had the same texture. In fact, our environment is composed of an incredible number and variety of textural surfaces. Our paintings should exhibit our sensitivity to texture and its marvelous variety.

ACTUAL
TEXTURES IN
NATURE

ACTUAL
TEXTURES IN
ACRYLIC AND
OIL PAINTINGS

IMPLIED
TEXTURES IN
WATERCOLOR
PAINTINGS

ACTUAL AND
IMPLIED TEXTURES
IN WATERCOLOR AND
COLLAGE PAINTINGS

USING COLLAGE TO ENHANCE TEXTURE

Textural effects and surface enrichment are implicit goals of artists working with collage. Although many kinds of manufactured and handmade papers can be used to satisfy these goals, Oriental papers are generally the most visually and tactilely stimulating. They not only provide the desired surface enrichment, but can also lead artists in unanticipated directions.

There are two basic ways to start the collage process. You can adhere Oriental papers directly to a surface, without painting the surface first. This produces a textured white or off-white ground, depending on the papers used as collage material. When dry, this textured ground can be painted with watercolors or other water media, and further enriched with pencils, Prismacolors, or pastels.

As discussed in the previous chapters, you can also adhere Oriental papers over watercolor washes so that color shows through the collaged papers, providing basic tones for the subsequent painting. When color shows through the more translucent papers, it tends to accentuate the textural qualities of the various papers by allowing the embedded fibers to stand out. It also emphasizes the layering process.

COLLAGING ON UNPAINTED WATERCOLOR PAPER

COLLAGING ON PAINTED WATERCOLOR PAPER

Left Column:

Torn Oriental papers are collaged directly on unpainted watercolor paper. When watercolor is applied over the collaged surface, it lies on top of the collaged papers. A second layer of watercolor is brushed over the surface, enriching textures and providing a layered effect.

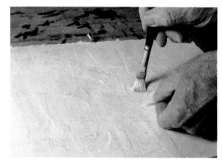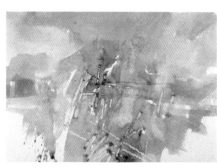

Right Column:

Watercolor is first brushed freely on watercolor paper to give it a basic tone. When Oriental papers are collaged over the painted ground, some color shows through the collaged papers. Finally, when watercolor is brushed over the collaged surface, there is a layered effect, with color still evident through the papers.

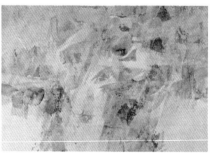

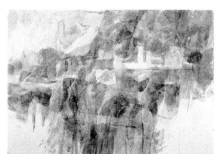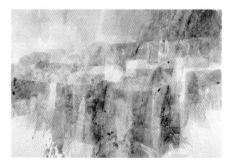

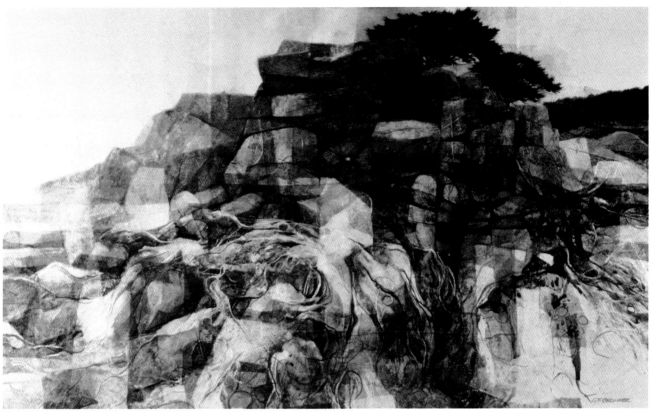

CARMEL IMPRESSION/TIDE POOLS. Watercolor and collage on Strathmore board, 22" × 30" (56 × 76 cm). Courtesy of Fireside Gallery, Carmel, California.

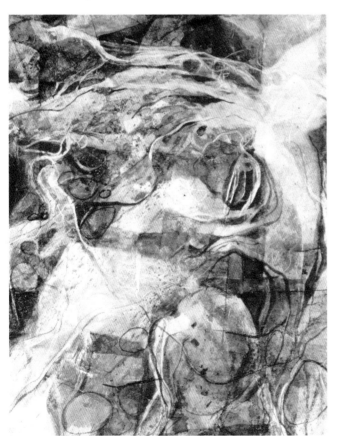

This painting was begun with a bold, free application of color to suggest the typical rock patterns found along the Carmel coast. Areas of sloshing water were left white. Then Oriental papers were collaged over the rock and water areas, but not over the sky, which became an untextured foil for the impressive coastal textures. Later, trees were added to provide further contrast for the rocky elements. Observe how the dark and light shafts seem to weave the surface together, unifying otherwise disparate elements.

In the detail you can see how paint has been applied to accentuate the natural textures in the papers. Some painted passages and lines are keyed to existing collage elements, while others are deliberately designed to unite the surface elements. Note the transitional passages from negative to positive spaces, and the use of collage to help suggest distance, space, movement, and texture. In some areas the collage is left completely visible and unpainted, while in other areas the watercolor almost obliterates the textural qualities of the collaged papers.

LAYERING PAPERS FOR MULTIPLE TEXTURES

Artists who use transparent media often lay one color over another to produce a surface that is infinitely richer in color than if a single wash were used. Collage artists can also take advantage of layering. It can be visually stimulating to apply papers over each other, producing a more richly textured ground.

By layering papers, you can actually create new surface textures: one type of texture glued over a second yields a third texture, which includes some of both characteristics. Experiment to find papers that help construct an interesting surface on which to build your painting. Be sure, however, that the first paper is relatively dry before collaging another paper on top—otherwise, you will have to wait a long time for the bottom layer to dry completely.

Layering can also enhance unity. Often it is essential to collage pieces of lightweight paper over parts of a surface to tie together papers with disparate physical characteristics.

By using thin papers with visible fibers, you can create a common visual bond, uniting the surface elements.

When you layer the papers, be sure that all edges and corners are completely adhered to prevent unwanted splotching and darkened areas. It is not necessary to add heavy brushloads of glue over the papers to make them stick firmly to the ground. You may, however, wish to brush or spray thin coats of diluted acrylic medium (about a 50/50 mixture) over the collaged surface, after it is dry. Wait until this brushed surface is completely dry before applying watercolor washes. Experiment on small swatches to determine the best mixtures and the most desirable surfaces.

The number of paper layers is not restricted in any way. You can add a layer or two as the painting is progressing to reintroduce light areas or to provide heavier or lighter textures. As long as the surface is dry, you can add layers as often as necessary to produce the desired result.

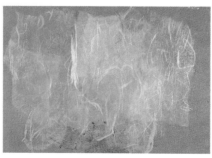
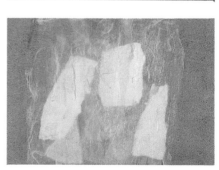

Different Oriental papers (left) and 300 lb., 140 lb., and Oriental papers (right) have been collaged on a painted watercolor sheet.

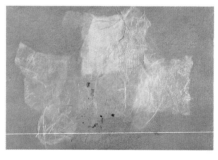
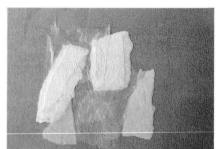

Additional Oriental papers are collaged over the two surfaces.

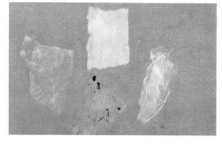
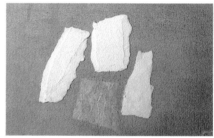

Now a single type of Oriental paper is collaged over the different papers to provide a homogeneous surface.

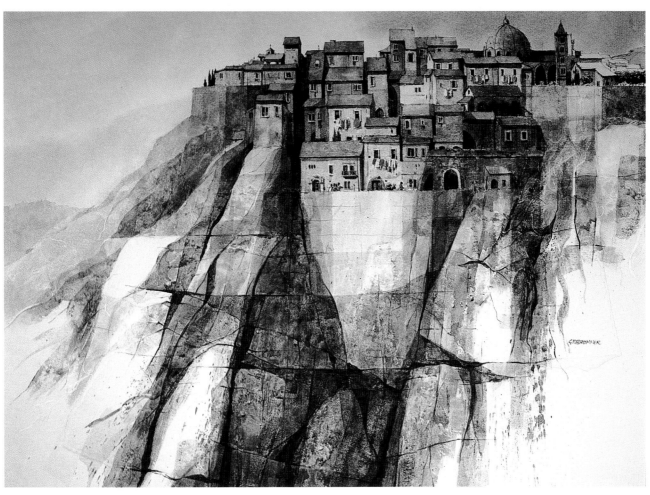

WINTER HILLTOWN/TUSCANY. Watercolor and collage, 22" × 30" (56 × 76 cm).
Collection of Mr. and Mrs. Harvey Bookstein.

Wet-in-wet washes form a soft backdrop for the heavy textures featured in this
painting. After blocking in the general shape of the hillside on the dry surface, I
used a pencil to delineate the structures perched atop the jagged cliffs. I then
glued large chunks of 300 lb. rough paper to the cliff shapes and let the torn
edges suggest crevices and gorges. After layering Oriental papers over the
remaining parts of the town and cliffs, I began to paint. Later, I layered more
Oriental papers onto the cliffs, covering some of the previously applied papers.
This textural buildup of the surface began to suggest the centuries of crumbling
and weathering of the cliffs. By extending the dark and light shapes into the
perched village, I visually cemented it to the craggy hillside.

ADDING EFFECTIVE BRUSHWORK

The textures of handmade Oriental papers become integral parts of the paintings in which they are used. Color washes brushed over them often emphasize and enhance their textures. The amount of adhesive used and the evenness of its application also influence the textural surface, as does any glue or acrylic medium brushed over or left on the surface.

In addition, brushmarks made on the textured ground can influence the quality of the collaged surface. It is truly remarkable to watch what happens when a single, wide brushstroke comes from a flat, softhair brush. Caressing a 1-inch or ¾-inch brush, partially dried with an absorbent tissue, over the textured surface will produce breathtaking results. Many times, nothing else need be done in certain areas. Further glazes, however, may enhance the initial washes.

A pointed brush can also be used, to increase the texture in selected areas. Where the collaged papers have produced a rather flat color area, you can add texture just as in direct watercolor painting—making dots, squiggles, or calligraphic lines. The side of a partially loaded brush will pick up the relief of the Oriental papers and emphasize their textures. Using the fibers and textures of the collaged papers as a starting point, you can duplicate, alter, elongate, outline, or otherwise emphasize the natural surface qualities or invent implied textures of your own.

With a pointed brush, fan brush, or toothbrush, you can spatter color on parts of the surface to create finely dotted textures. Often these painted textures combine with the paper textures to create wonderfully complex surfaces.

A sponge can also be used in several ways to work with texture. Dip small pieces of a natural or manufactured sponge in color and print on top of the collaged surface. Or use the sponge to remove part of the applied watercolor and produce still different kinds of texture.

With absorbent tissues, you can blot color and enhance certain textural effects. If too much color is applied, and textures are lost, blotting and lifting may permit textures to emerge. By wiping with tissues and scraping with a chisel-handled brush, you can also lift some wet color and thereby create different kinds of surface marks and textures.

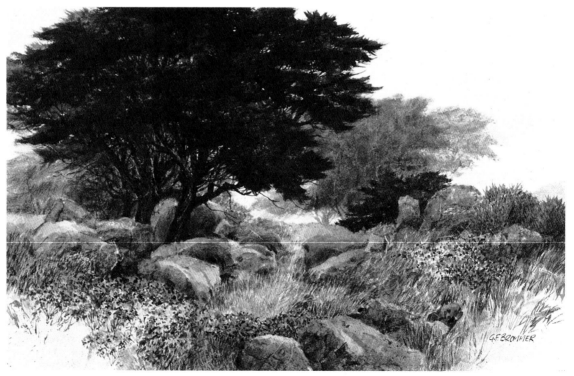

MISTY MEADOW/CARMEL. Watercolor and collage, 15" × 22" (38 × 56 cm). Collection of Mr. William Woods.

Watercolor marks, applied to a textured ground with a pointed brush, result in indications of grass, bushes, flowers, tree branches, foliage, and rock crevices.

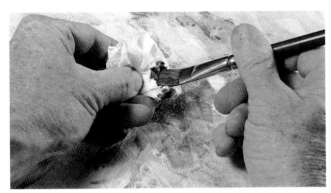

Before applying watercolor to a collaged surface, remove some liquid color from the brush by blotting it on an absorbent tissue.

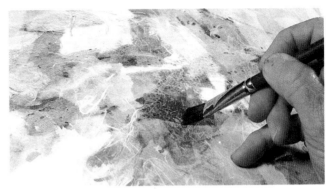

Take a flat brush, partially dried, and lay down a colored wash to emphasize the textures of collaged papers.

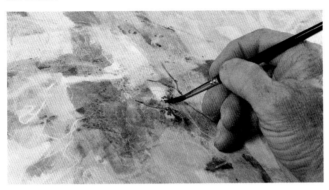

Use a pointed brush to draw lines, dots, and squiggles.

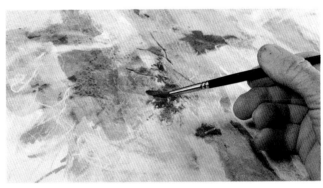

Scrumble with the side of a partially dried brush to produce textures that reflect the low relief of collaged papers.

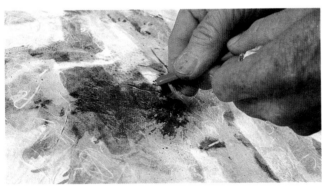

Spatter watercolor with a toothbrush on the collaged surface, adding dot-patterned textures.

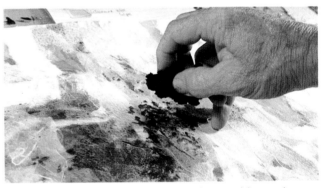

Print with a sponge dipped in watercolor to add organic marks to an already textural surface.

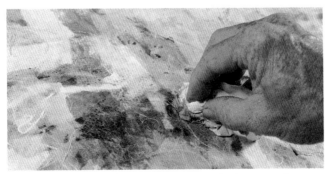

Blot with absorbent tissue to create new textures or wipe away color with the tissue, revealing the papers' fibrous textures.

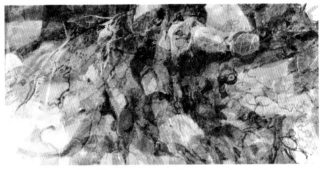

Experiment with different kinds of brushmarks to introduce specific textural patterns to the collaged surface.

INTRODUCING OTHER MATERIALS

With collage, there are many directions that artists may explore. Oriental papers are made in many colors and patterns, and some of these can be advantageous in various situations. Experiment with different handmade papers or try adhering lightweight watercolor paper, different kinds of Bristol paper, and charcoal paper to heavy surfaces, such as 300 or 400 lb. paper, watercolor board, or paper mounted on Masonite. You can also use several kinds of fabric as accent textures, or shred the ends of cloth material to expose loose threads and fibers.

Try staining Oriental papers *before* gluing them to the surface, by applying watercolor or acrylic paints with a large softhair brush, and allowing them to dry completely before collaging them. Then, instead of watercolor, use thinned casein, or stain the papers with any medium on both sides for varying effects. Remain flexible when it comes to developing experimental surfaces.

Some papers can be decollaged—that is, parts can be torn and removed from the collaged surface. Bristol paper and some kinds of watercolor paper can be slit and ripped to create wonderful edges, which absorb paint differently from normal surfaces. You can do this before or after applying paint to the collaged surface.

Opaque paints can be thinned and used to create a different kind of surface, following the same techniques as for watercolors. Try caseins, gouaches, and acrylics. You can then apply transparent watercolors over the casein or gouache, if you do not wait too long for the surface to harden. They will not work over acrylics, however, unless the acrylics have been thinned drastically. If white gesso (made from Gesso Ground Dry Mixture) is used to opaque collaged areas (either heavily or lightly), watercolor will still adhere to the painted surface.

To create a resistant area, draw or mark with white crayon or candle wax before running watercolor washes over the collaged surface. Pencil, charcoal, crayon, or pastels can also be used on the textured surfaces before or after painting with watercolor. The list of possible combinations of media and techniques seems almost endless and allows for personal exploration and expression in many varied directions.

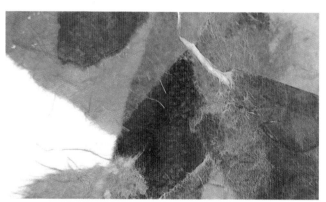

Stained Oriental papers glow when overlapped and glued to a white sheet, but they retain their identifying characteristics.

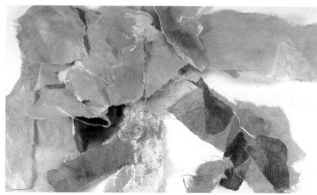

This pile of watercolor-stained Oriental papers is ready for collaging.

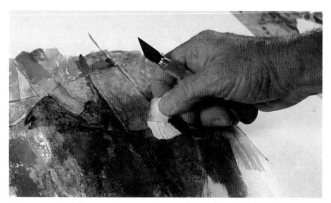

You can decollage a layer of two-ply, painted Bristol paper after slitting the edge with a knife.

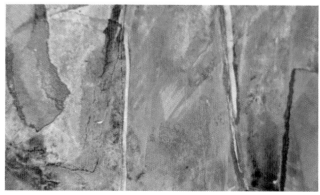

Here watercolor is applied over a collage surface of torn pieces of Bristol paper and 300 lb. watercolor paper.

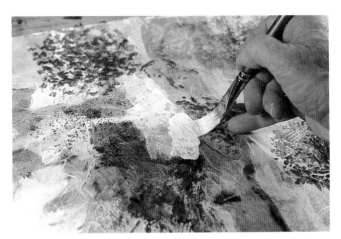

Try brushing diluted white gouache over a painted and collaged surface.

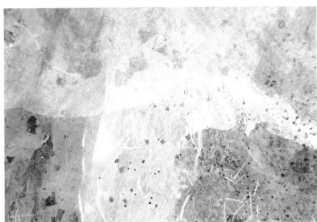

It is difficult to tell the difference between opaque Oriental paper (top) and diluted opaque gouache brushed over collaged papers (bottom).

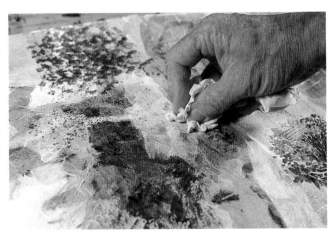

An absorbent tissue can be used to wipe excess white gouache from the collaged surface.

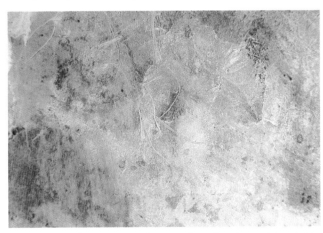

A misty veil of white gouache remains after the moist paint is wiped off immediately after application.

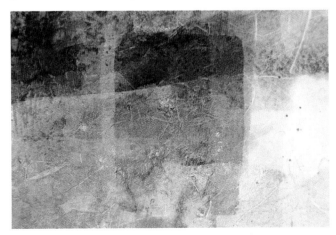

Colors and textures show through a thin veil of white gouache, which has been partially wiped off.

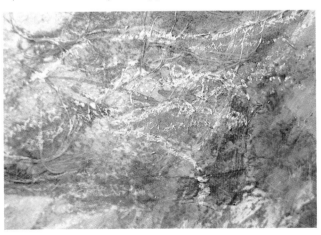

White wax crayon lines resist additional watercolor washes and provide new textures.

TAKING ADVANTAGE OF THE WATERCOLOR PAPER SURFACE

In collaging Oriental papers to watercolor paper, not all of the watercolor sheet has to be covered in every painting. Sometimes the watercolor paper surface itself is helpful in completing the painting concept. You might, for example, want a large area of a single, dark color to describe a dark sky, smooth water, or a grove of dark green trees. Such an area is often best treated as an uncollaged surface, because if torn paper is visible, it may interfere with the intended evenness.

It is also often advantageous to work a textured area against a smooth area, creating a contrast. The textures of a pile of rocks, for example, will be more effective against a smooth sky than against another textured mountain. Flower textures may be enhanced if seen against an untextured background. Painted or unpainted watercolor paper can be an excellent foil for collaged and textured subject matter, as well as for positive shapes.

At times, however, you may want a transitional passage, linking a textured and a nontextured surface. This allows the eye to move freely from one to the other without being stopped abruptly by a strong, contrasting edge. You can create a transitional passage by using close values in places where textured and nontextured areas meet. Or you can tear heavily fibered papers and allow the fibers to tie the textured and nontextured areas together, both visually and physically. This device can be extremely effective in vignettes or partial vignettes, and it can provide initial visual movement from negative space into the more completely articulated parts of a painting.

For a balance between textured and nontextured areas, plan to include areas of heavy texture, light texture, and no texture in your collage, just as you would in a direct watercolor. This is not a firm rule, however, and you may break it or adjust it to visually articulate the effect or mood you intend.

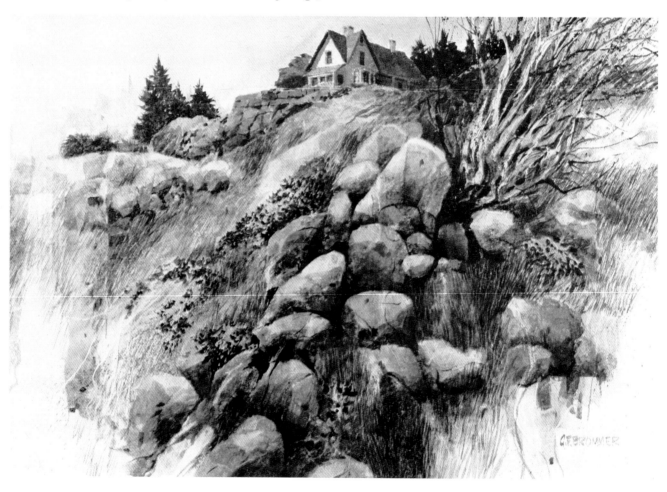

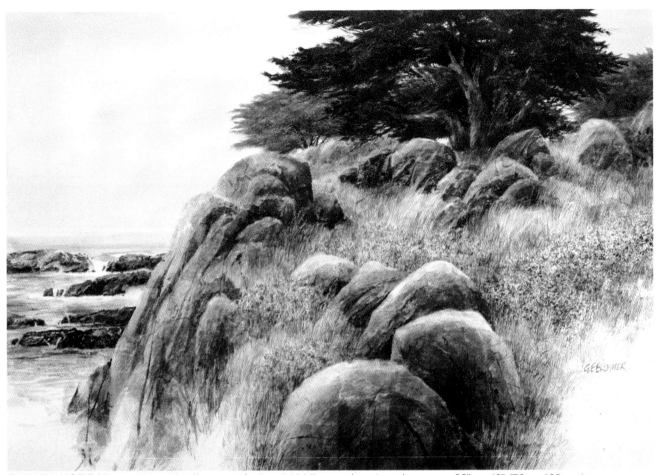

CARMEL MOTIF. Watercolor and collage, on Arches 1114 lb. rough watercolor paper, 30" × 40" (76 × 102 cm). Collection of Imperial Savings Association, San Diego, California.

In this large painting, the foggy sky area is not collaged, and neither is the foliage of the trees. The remainder of the surface is covered with Oriental papers, except for the white corners in the foreground. The flatness of the sky area increases interest in the textured surface of the painting. Because the values are nearly equal in the flat sky and the textured rocks and ocean, they are visually tied together.

Note the transitions, which allow visual movement from the negative spaces in the bottom corners to the positive areas. Although collaged papers can be seen in these transitional passages, they do not dominate. Also observe how the rocks were painted to take advantage of the paper textures, while pointed brushes were used to develop the grass and flower areas, painted over the collaged surface.

SIERRA SPRING. Watercolor and collage, 15" × 22" (38 × 56 cm). Collection of Doug Ostroski.

The house, background trees, and sky were not collaged in this painting, nor were the bottom corners. The textured areas thus received added emphasis because of their contrast with these uncollaged spaces. Notice the transitional areas from the sky to the hill and from the corners into the subject. The high horizon emphasizes the verticality of this composition, even though it is painted on a horizontal half-sheet. Rocks, trees, and grass accentuate this upward visual thrust, which culminates in the house perched atop the rocky hill.

PERSONAL APPROACHES TO TEXTURE

Collage techniques encourage an individual approach to painting and allow you to make a personal statement with your art. The three artists whose work is shown on these two pages have all used watercolor and collage techniques to create unique images. The work of these and other artists in this book emphasizes the freedom the medium allows and the delightful individuality it fosters.

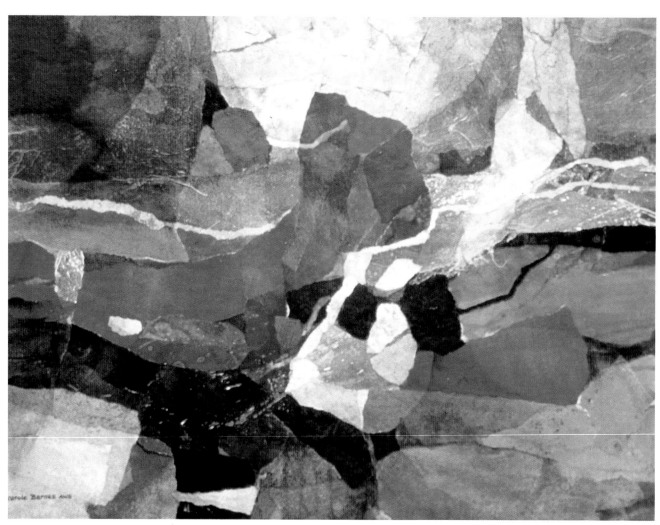

COASTAL COVE, by Carole Barnes. Watercolor, acrylic, and collage, 21" × 27" (53 × 69 cm). Private collection.

This artist often begins with abstractly painted shapes, collage, and color and manipulates these elements until they suggest a subject. She then enhances this subject with further collage and painting. In the work shown here, rocks, water, and cliffs are suggested but remain abstracted symbols as the colored shapes play against each other across the collaged surface. Many of the colored shapes were torn from acrylic-stained papers and adhered to the surface. White Oriental papers and white acrylic paint were used for accents, and watercolor glazes provide a delicate translucency, in strong contrast to the opaque shapes.

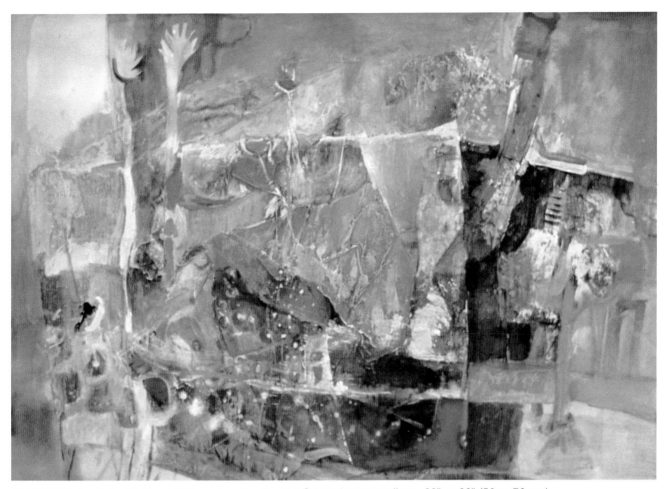

BLUE REEF, by Helen B. Reed. Watercolor, acrylic, and Oriental paper collage, 22" × 30" (56 × 76 cm). Collection of the artist.

Although at first glance this painting has the quality of an abstract still life arrangement, the cool, underwater colors and textures suggest pieces of a reef in a South Pacific lagoon. There is a blue-green color dominance, but the textures emerge as the most important feature. Inside a balanced, vertically and horizontally oriented composition, colors dance in excited rhythms, pushed relentlessly by the collaged surface. Oriental papers of many types reveal their textural characteristics, and the way the artist has applied watercolor and acrylic paint emphasizes them.

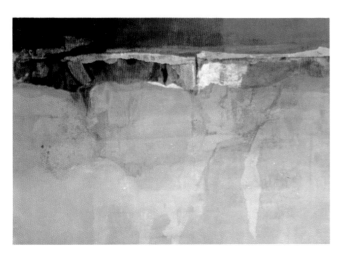

STRATA V, by Pauline Doblado. Transparent and opaque watercolor and collage, 20" × 26" (51 × 66 cm). Private collection.

As this painting was developing, the artist felt it lacked strength and depth, so she tore pieces from an old watercolor painting on 300 lb. paper and glued them in a band across the upper part of the sheet. She combined these with pieces of Oriental paper and let everything dry. Next she painted a band of flowing watercolor across the top of the sheet and allowed it to run into the collaged areas, creating fascinating textures. After mixing a puddle of opaque gray, she brushed it over the bottom two-thirds of the sheet, where it acted as a translucent veil. When it was dry, subtle shapes beneath the veil emerged, directing visual movement to the more complex, textural band.

5
USING LINE EFFECTIVELY

In paintings where texture is the dominant element of design, it might seem that line would play a relatively unimportant part. In some cases that may be true, but artists who use line as a major element in their direct painting techniques can also use line effectively when working with watercolor and collage.

One way to use line is to take advantage of the embedded fibers contained in many Oriental papers. Some papers have long, stringy fibers while others contain short, bristly fibers. Some fibers are thin while others are wide; some are single while others are multiple. These fibers read as line when the papers are collaged to the painting surface. They can be made more important by the way the papers are painted, or reduced in their importance. White fibers on white watercolor paper, for example, can enrich negative space or serve as transitions between the negative and positive areas of a painting.

If you want details in your painting, you can draw pencil or pen-and-ink lines under or over collaged papers. With colored pencils or Prismacolors, you can develop color areas or outline, separate, or sketch subjects in the painting. Similarly, with pastels and watercolor crayons, you can add color areas or make colored lines on collaged surfaces. Try brushing watercolor washes over them to produce different results. If, on the other hand, you use wax crayons to make lines and textures, they will resist any watercolor applied over them, creating still different effects.

To modify any of these linear marks even further, collage thin or medium-weight Oriental papers over them. Then make marks on top of these collaged papers to create the effect of layered lines. Combining lines and watercolor washes with textured surfaces opens up many possible directions and concepts for you to explore.

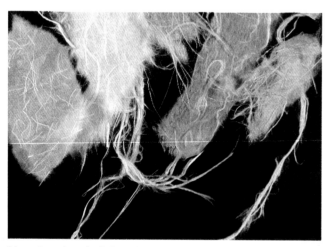

Many handmade Oriental papers already have lines in them—in the form of embedded fibers. These fibers may vary in width, length, color, complexity, and strength.

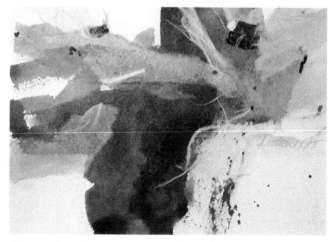

When collaged over watercolor, these fibered papers can create white lines on the surface. In this detail, the white lines contrast with the painted surface, with stained papers, and with other, unstained Oriental papers.

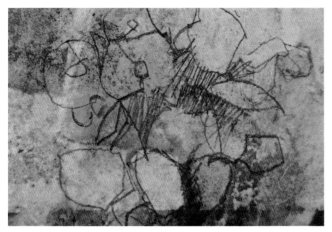

Pencil lines are easily drawn on a collaged surface, because the texture of the papers acts like the tooth of a fine drawing paper. The lines may serve as sketch lines for further painting or become integral parts of the design or texture itself.

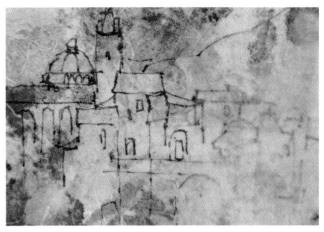

The lines in this detail were made over a collaged surface with a Speedball C-6 pen point and a mixture of sepia and india inks. They have an etched quality. On the right, they are seen through a layer of paper collaged over them.

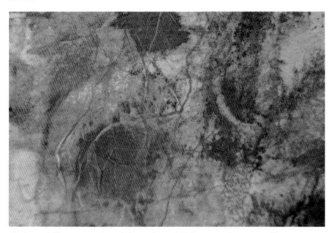

Colored lines made with pointed Prismacolor pencils are opaque and can be used over darker values. When the side of the pencil is used, the textured papers respond individually, with different results. Finer lines can be made by using regular colored pencils.

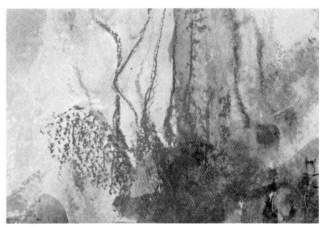

Watercolor crayons make colored lines and shaded areas that look like they were made with wax crayons. But when water is brushed over them (right), the colors are diluted and spread, appearing as watercolor washes.

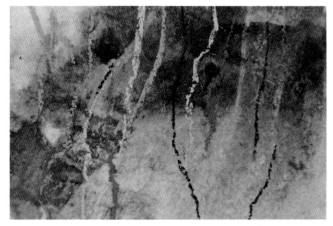

Lines made with the edge of a pastel stick will show up vividly on a dark area. Such lines should be added at the end of the working process and sprayed with fixative to keep them from smudging.

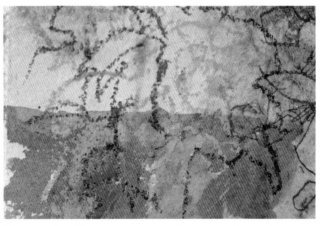

Lines made with a wax crayon resist watercolor washes applied over them (bottom). With or without the addition of watercolor, these lines can produce exciting textures on collaged surfaces.

EXPERIMENTING WITH BRUSHED LINES

Pointed brushes of various types are capable of making the most magnificent lines in all of painting. And the organic quality of a brushed line can mesh beautifully with the textural characteristics of a collaged surface, especially if Oriental papers are involved. You should experiment with different brushes and varied amounts of water and color, however, because the collaged surface is not as absorbent as a pristine watercolor sheet.

Try using your brush to outline shapes or objects in a collage painting. Or let the brush meander over the surface to create a calligraphic statement independent of existing shapes. Explore different qualities of line: thin or fat, straight or curvilinear, light or dark, continuous or intermittent. Use these lines to separate or join areas; let them lie inert or make them dance about the surface, directing visual movement throughout the painting.

When you brush lines on a collaged surface, you can key them to existing fibers or paper edges, creating linear patterns within the painting. In this case, the painted lines actually become part of the collaged surface, enhancing the textural qualities of the Oriental papers. But you can also use brushed lines to enhance the subject matter. You might, for example, delineate the details in structures or plants with brushed lines that are independent of the textural surface. Or you might mass lines together to suggest tall grasses, tumbling water, tree trunks, or weathered boards.

As you explore these different possibilities, pay attention to how line can help you to communicate your thoughts and feelings about your subject. Of course, superb watercolor and collage paintings can be built without line, but many collagists use brushed lines as a dynamic and integral element in their work.

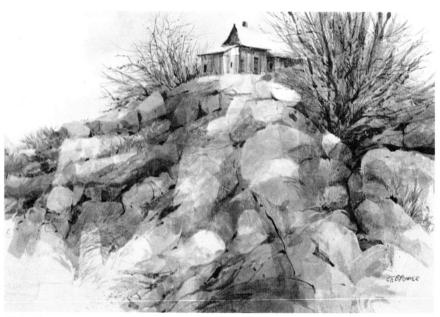

HIGH COUNTRY/SNOW AND ROCKS. Watercolor and collage, 15″ × 22″ (38 × 56 cm). Collection of Mr. and Mrs. William Gelb.

Color shapes and a variety of brushed lines dominate this painting of a simple subject—a house on a hill. The most obvious lines are those that suggest the trunks and branches of the winter trees. Some of these lines are derived from collaged fibers, but others are not. Lines are also used to articulate the boulders that compose the hill. In most cases, these are intermittent lines; they do not outline rocks, but emphasize the shadows and crevices, allowing passage from rock to rock. Notice that in some places the fibers of collaged papers act as white lines. Also observe the colored lines that indicate the dried winter grasses on the hill and the textures in the boards and shadows of the house.

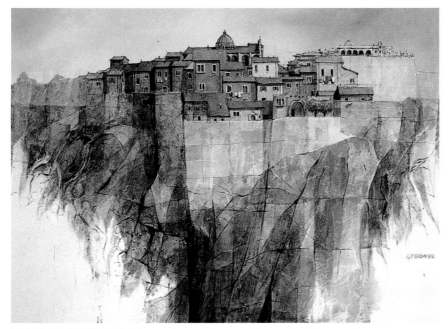

Line plays a dual role in this impression of a perched village in Italy. It extends the fibers and acts as a transition between the negative and positive spaces in the lower half of the painting. But it also delineates portions of the buildings clustered atop the ragged cliff. Dark watercolor lines outline and suggest windows, doorways, rooftops, and the ubiquitous lines of drying clothes. White lines, made with opaque gouache, emphasize window shapes and simulate the marble trim found in such villages. Some horizontal lines in the lower portion of the painting are used to tie the facets of the cliff together and echo the horizontal emphasis in the village above.

UMBRIAN HILLTOWN. Watercolor, white gouache, and collage, 15" × 22" (38 × 56 cm). Collection of Charles Duevel, III.

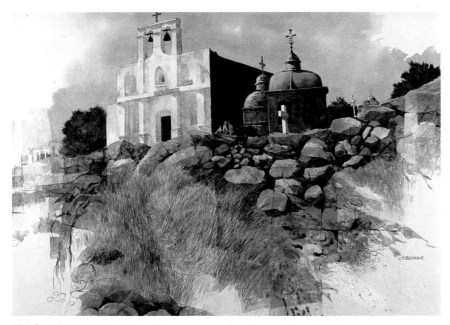

Lines fulfill a variety of functions in this painting of an old Sonoran mission in northern Mexico. Massed together, colored lines create the feeling of drying grass on the rocky slope. Line describes the contours of some rocks; in other places it is arbitrary and breaks up space and light. On the lower right, lines provide a calligraphic transition from the negative space to the solid rocks, while on the lower left lines serve as extensions of the fibers of collaged papers. Notice the many areas of passage and the ways that light provides movement within the painting.

KINO MISSION/OQUITOA. Watercolor and collage, 22" × 30" (56 × 76 cm) Private collection.

EXPLORING LINE,
TEXTURE, AND COLLAGE

This painting is the third in a series dealing with the famous Cannery Row in Monterey, California. The first two paintings created the illusion of depth and space through traditional linear and aerial perspective. In this painting, however, the structural elements are turned slightly to face the viewer, so they present a series of flat panels receding in space. This geometric concept is then strengthened by the collage process itself, as papers are applied in a general vertical and horizontal direction. The use of line also reinforces this idea.

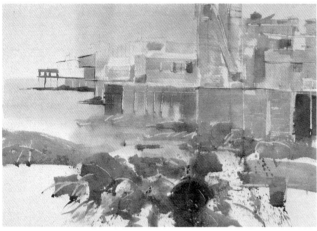

Pencil lines establish the basic layout and positioning of the structures and rocks. Flat planes are stacked one behind the other and establish a geometric concept. Light values of local color are quickly brushed in to set initial color relationships; they are allowed to dry before the collage process begins.

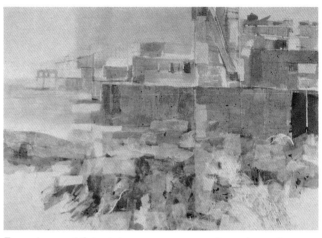

Torn pieces of Oriental paper are now collaged over the underlying colors. Areas that will feature texture are given a solid covering, as papers overlap and build up. Not all the surface is collaged, however. The foggy sky and distant water are left uncollaged, to act as a flat contrast to the textured foreground. Already the general vertical and horizontal application of the papers is determining the geometric outcome of the painting.

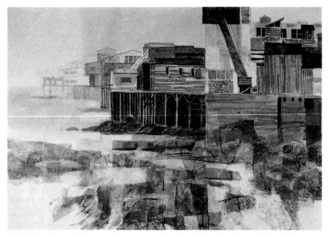

Initial watercolor washes, applied with a drybrush technique, begin to suggest the ultimate color and value relationships. More important, they reflect the geometric structural concept. Lines and edges in the foreground rocks and water are keyed to the established edges in the structures. Distant buildings are purposely kept light in value to suggest foggy distance.

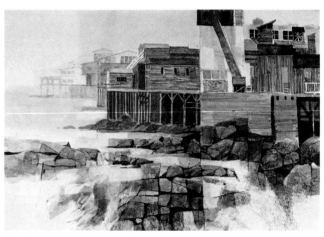

As the rocky foreground is developed, the crevices and spaces between rocks are lined up with the vertical edges above. In some places, lines are keyed to the paper edges, but they are also used to strengthen the geometric concept. This cubistic effect is becoming the dominant visual theme.

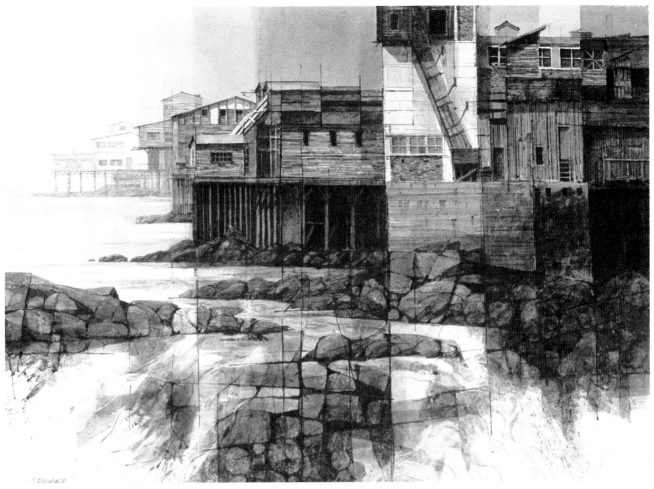

*MONTEREY DESIGN/CANNERY ROW. Watercolor and collage on Arches 300 lb.
cold-pressed paper, 22" × 30" (56 × 76 cm). Collection of Mr. and Mrs. Robert McNulty.*

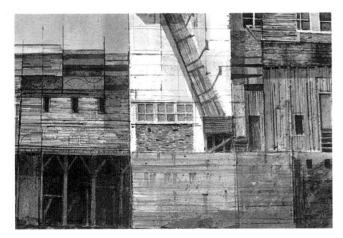

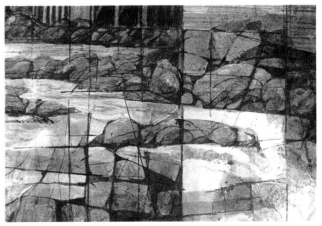

In final stages, values are adjusted and strengthened to emphasize the shaftlike panels and to provide a sense of space, moving back and forth, on the patterned surface. Notice the vital importance of line in the work. Lines that reinforce the abstract structure are evident, but so are lines that extend the flow of fibers and act as transitional elements. Some lines are left as lines, while others become shapes, crevices, rocks, water, boards, windows. This ambiguity develops visual tension, creating a dynamic interplay among the visual elements.

PERSONAL APPROACHES TO LINE

Obviously, line can be used in many ways in working with collaged surfaces. In the work shown on these pages, line describes shapes, establishes edges, and also exists independently, running over colors and shapes. The different ways the artists use line indicate something of their individual styles of communication. While the collage process helped determine their use of line, their lines in turn reflect their personal responses to the collage process.

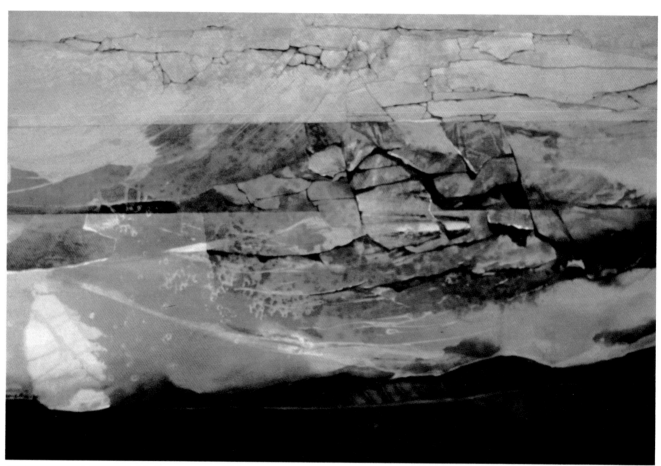

ANCIENT WALL SERIES #6, by Katherine Chang Liu. Acrylic and collage on Strathmore watercolor board, 30" × 40" (76 × 102 cm). Private collection.

This painting is one of a series in which the artist explored the themes of grandeur and decay, time and space, as expressed in the remains of ancient walls. Once the basic wall structure was established, she painted chips of various papers, including Oriental, watercolor, Bristol, and tissue papers, and collaged them to create textures or contrasts of color and value. Using acrylics, she was able to lay transparent glazes over opaque areas. To emphasize the feeling of weathering and decay, she used line to indicate chipped rocks, crevices, and cracks. Some of these lines are keyed to the collaged papers, while others are painted to create shapes independent of the added papers, although they continue the pattern the papers establish.

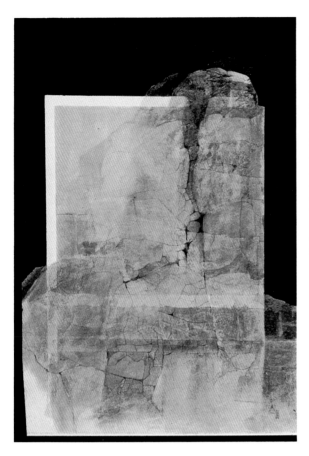

EREHWON II, by Marge Moore. Watercolor and collage, 30" × 22" (76 × 56 cm). Private collection.

The rocky image in this painting was not predetermined by the artist. Initially she used tape to isolate the outside border and painted it with a strong, flat, dark value, which acts as a foil for the textures of the collage. She then applied pale watercolor washes to the interior to establish color dominance. When they were dry, she collaged the surface with torn pieces of several kinds of Oriental paper and allowed them to dry completely. Then she pulled thin watercolor glazes over the collaged surface until interesting shapes began to emerge. Moore purposely kept the washes high-keyed and transparent to emphasize the papers' textures and to contrast with the dark border. When the torn paper edges suggested rock formations, she added the delicate linear pattern. By keeping the lines light and subtle, she made sure the emphasis remained on the transparency of the textured, rocky surface—an evident ambiguity.

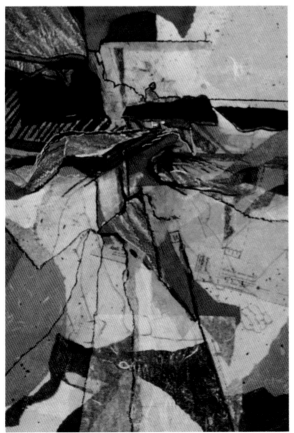

CELEBRATING THE EARTH, by Valaida D'Alessio. Mixed water media and collage, 30" × 22" (76 × 56 cm). Private collection.

The layering of papers, colors, and lines is evident in this painting. Some papers retain their characteristic textural identities, while others are obscured by paint, pattern, or other papers. Opaque and marbled papers are used in combination with Oriental papers and transparent and opaque water media to establish a richly textured surface. Line is introduced as pattern, as a delineation of paper edges, and as an independent element, cavorting about the surface. Lines are also layered, with some seen under Oriental papers and others atop them. The lines are intriguing because of their varied weights, values, colors, textures, and purposes, as well as the different media used to make them.

6
SOURCES OF VISUAL INFORMATION

Since artists are visual communicators, most rely on visual stimulation to trigger their creative energies. Some artists paint directly from nature, people, or objects, while others sketch first and then make paintings based on their sketches. Some like to photograph their subjects and use prints or slides as the basis for their paintings; still others rely on imagination or memory to provide the raw material for their paintings. Some artists may even use one or more of their own paintings as visual stimulation for additional works in an ongoing series.

Artists working with watercolor and collage make use of the same resources for visual information. They can also use the collage itself as information, relying on it to suggest possible colors, shapes, lines, and subjects. Of course, how the artist then develops the painting will vary from individual to individual. The examples shown in this chapter are just that—examples. They are not meant to be the ultimate answer for every artist. Use them as suggestions and fill in the missing steps as you experiment and explore the variety of options.

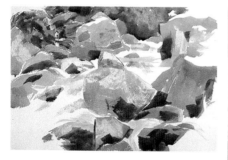

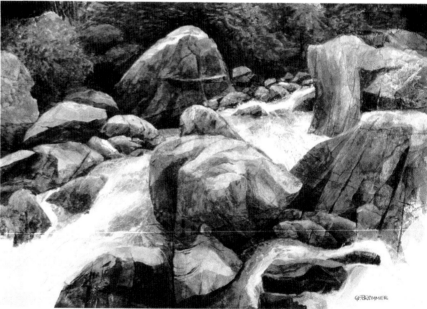

ROCKS AND WATER/MERCED RIVER. Watercolor and collage, 15″ × 22″ (38 × 56 cm). Private collection.

For my basic "start," I painted quickly and freely on location, without sketching or drawing on the sheet. It was a direct response to the subject. Then, in the studio, I collaged torn Oriental papers over the entire surface and painted the subject (as I remembered it) over the textured ground. As I worked, the painting itself suggested where modifications and adjustments were needed in the design. It was more important to relate the various parts of the painting to each other than to duplicate the image seen in nature.

WORKING DIRECTLY FROM THE SUBJECT

You may wish to go right to nature for your source material, and you can do this by beginning your work on location. You probably have your favorite methods for painting on location, but typically artists begin by making a series of sketches to determine the composition and center of interest. Then a pencil or a brush can be used to sketch the major elements on the watercolor sheet. You need not develop the painting in detail because much of it will be covered in the ensuing collage process. Large washes of local color suffice for a beginning. This "start" can be taken back to the studio for collaging and further development. To remember details in the scene, you can draw in your sketchbook or take photographs, although you can also rely on your memory or imagination. If portions of the work will not be collaged, you may want to work on those areas a bit more before going back to the studio.

If you enjoy working from still lifes, people, machinery, animals, or similar subjects, your procedure may be much the same. You may wish to sketch first to explore different ways of handling your subject. As you begin to paint, keep in mind that details will be covered by the collaged papers, so you need not waste time on them at this point. After you collage, you can draw in the details and continue the painting, or you may allow the developing painting to suggest further directions. Mix the working procedures described in previous chapters in developing your personal working techniques.

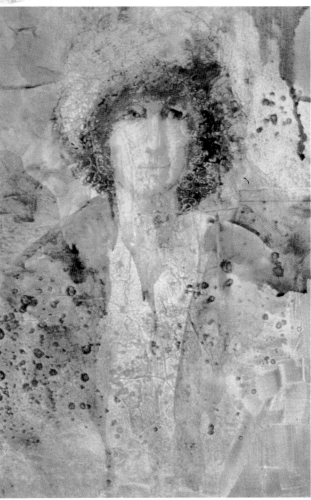

MARY, by Pauline Doblado. Watercolor, oil pastel, collage, and white gesso on watercolor board, 30″ × 24″ (76 × 61 cm). Private collection.

Pauline Doblado prepared the ground for this painting by applying white gesso and collaging torn Oriental papers on a watercolor board. She created a richly textured surface that was white and absorbent in varying degrees. After lightly drawing the portrait with oil pastels on this textured ground, she ran watercolor washes over the surface. Because of the alternate resisting (from the oil pastels) and absorbing, the colors emphasized the complex textures. Although the exact results could not be predicted, the artist retained control by selecting and using her materials with skill and care. Final touches with oil pastel and watercolor established the facial details and clinched the personal likeness.

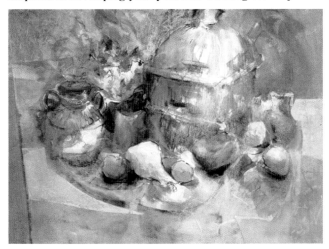

BLUE STILL LIFE, by Pat Lea. Watercolor, gesso, and collage, 22″ × 30″ (56 × 76 cm). Collection of the artist.

Pat Lea started this painting by drawing from a still life setup and adding watercolor washes in large, loose shapes. When this was dry, she brushed on white gesso in varying thicknesses to accentuate light values, establish movement, and provide surface unity. After this dried, she collaged torn Oriental papers in most of the positive areas to give the surface texture.

USING SLIDES AND PHOTOGRAPHS

While direct confrontation with subject matter is one of the finest art experiences, working from secondary sources is often essential, especially when studio techniques such as collage are used. Sketches, slides, photographs, and pictures from books and magazines are all viable visual resources. Indeed, most artists collect visual images, storing them in sophisticated filing systems or referring to boxes full of cluttered pictures. Artists use these images for help in understanding structure, remembering lighting conditions, or describing details. In addition to serving as memory joggers, these images can be idea stimulators, generating enthusiasm and setting creative wheels in motion.

Each artist establishes procedures for using these secondary sources in his or her painting process. Some may sketch from a slide or picture and then paint from the sketch. Others may project the slide image on paper and then draw or paint directly over the projection. No method works for all artists, so you must decide what is most comfortable for you.

Selective seeing is often important when you are using a photographic reference. The two examples shown on these pages reveal that liberties can be taken in arranging and painting subject matter based on slide images. If the same slides were used again to begin two more paintings, the final results would undoubtedly be different.

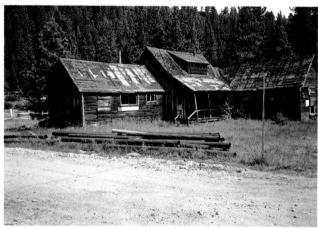

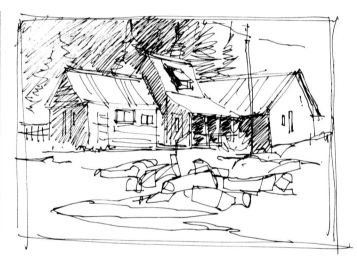

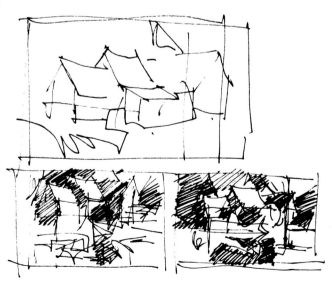

In the photograph of this old house in the California gold country, the buildings are very interesting, but the foreground is equally uninteresting. When I made a rough sketch from the slide (projected on a screen), I decided to change the pieces of pipe into logs. Then I explored the rough sketch further in several thumbnail drawings, trying different arrangements and value concepts. When the grouping and composition felt comfortable, I sketched the major elements and brushed on light values of local colors in large washes. With a second series of washes, I darkened some areas and arrived at a value pattern similar to that of the third small sketch.

Next, I collaged Oriental papers over the lower half of the painting and up into parts of the buildings. The sky, trees, hills, and portions of the buildings remained uncollaged. By painting watercolor over the collaged areas, I established the light pattern and united the lower and upper portions of the work. In doing this, I was influenced by the needs of the painting itself. The finished work resembles the slide and is derived from it, but does not imitate it in any way.

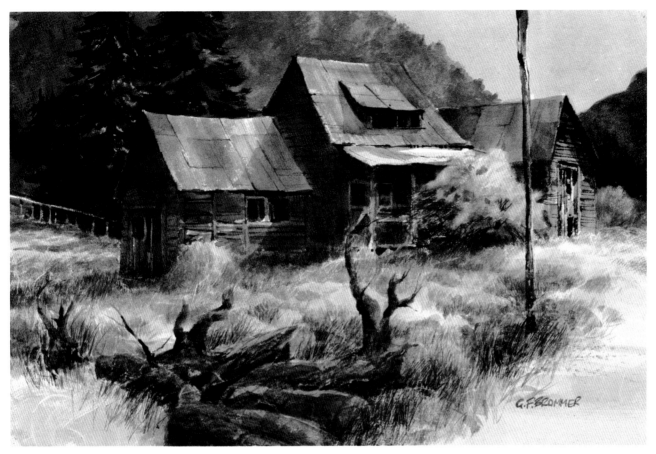

SIERRA HOMESTEAD. Watercolor and collage, 15" × 22"
(38 × 56 cm). Collection of Mr. and Mrs. Edward Pope.

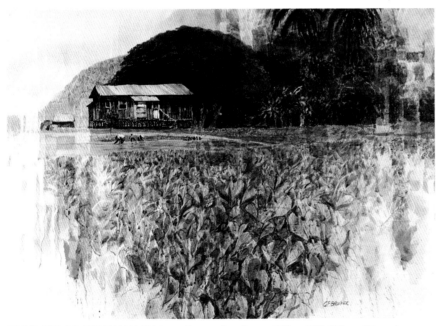

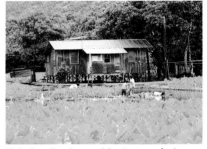

TARO FIELDS ON KAUAI. Watercolor and collage, 22" × 30" (56 × 76 cm).
Collection of Robert Maverick.

This fascinating subject was photo-graphed from a car window during a drenching Hawaiian rainstorm. I sketched the subject several times from the projected slide, and eventually decided to push the cottage up and back in the painting and emphasize the taro field, jungle, and rain. After drawing the major elements in pencil and laying in the initial washes (mostly greens), I collaged the entire surface. To convey the feeling of pouring rain, I glued the papers and fibers mostly in a vertical direction. The values—which range from cool, misty lights to dense, jungle darks—maintain this wet, rainy mood.

DEVELOPING IDEAS FROM SKETCHES

One of the traditional sources that artists use for visual information is the sketchbook. Often sketchbooks are visual treasure troves, loaded with picture-making ideas for years to come. The sketches themselves come in different forms—from rough ideas to detailed renderings, from contour line drawings to complete value studies, in pencil, ink, color, or marker. Some include written comments, while others record only visual imagery. No two sketchbooks look exactly alike, since they contain the personal visual notations of individual creative people.

Just as there are varieties of sketches, there are varieties of ways to use them. The examples shown on these pages are only two of many ways to use sketchbook references. Often artists combine photography and sketching to record visual information and rely on both to make complete statements.

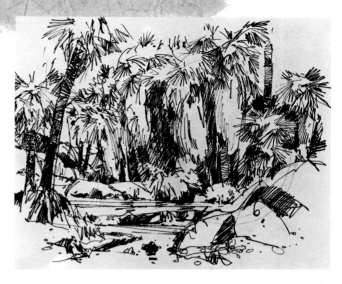

The sketch for Palm Canyon Stream, *drawn on location, provided all the visual material needed for the painting. I began the painting with a brush drawing, followed by light washes and collaged Oriental papers. When this was dry, I brushed on watercolor to develop the textures, shapes, and values described in the sketch. After a while, however, I stopped and abruptly changed everything—adding white gesso and more collaged papers to almost cover the surface* with whites. Then, by adding color again over the complex layering, I created the rich tactile quality of the finished painting. Note the many kinds of line used in the work, from calligraphic doodling to the careful rendering of the palm leaves. Also observe how the passage of light has been elaborated from the sketch so that it holds parts of the painting together and provides visual movement.

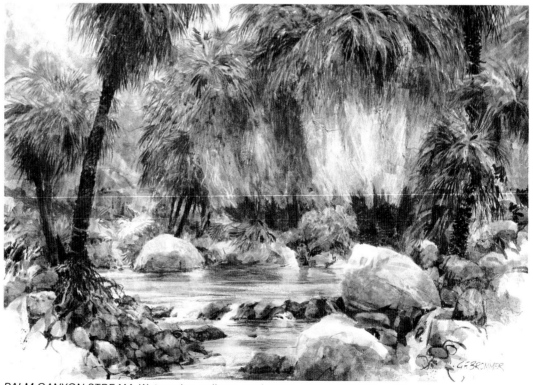

PALM CANYON STREAM. Watercolor, collage, and gesso, 22″ × 30″ (56 × 76 cm). Collection of Mr. and Mrs. David Perkins.

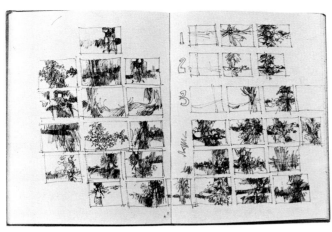

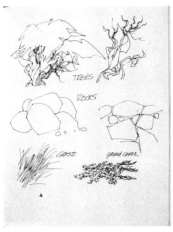

No actual visual resources were used for Carmel Impression. *Instead, it was based on the memory of previous painting experiences and designs worked out in a sketchbook. The process started with a number of small visual-concept sketches, strewn across two pages of my sketchbook. These sketches offered ideas for an entire series of paintings.*

To evoke the feeling of the Carmel area, I decided to use three basic elements: cypress trees, coastal rocks, and ground cover.

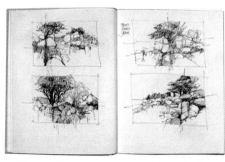

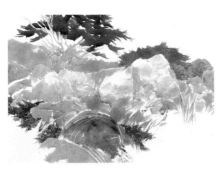

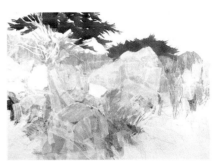

These elements were combined in four trial compositions based on designs found in the concept sketches.

After selecting one of these sketches, I drew the composition with pencil on the paper and then quickly brushed on light values of possible local colors.

Next, I collaged Oriental papers over everything except the trees and sky, and went on to finish the painting in the basic techniques already described.

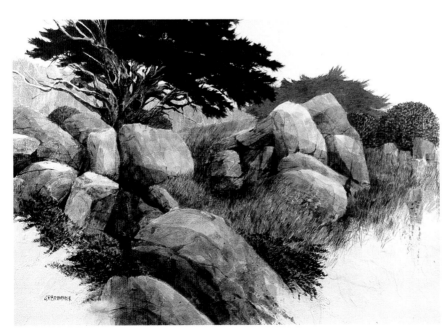

CARMEL IMPRESSION. Watercolor and collage, 15″ × 22″ (38 × 56 cm). Private collection.

Compare the finished painting with the sketches. Try a similar process, using a subject with which you are already familiar. Select a few simple elements and experiment with different arrangements to find a pleasing composition.

MAKING THE COLLAGE ITSELF A RESOURCE

We are constantly bombarded with visual information that suggests subject matter for our paintings. But there can also be an internal motivation—a drive that emanates from the developing painting itself. The marvelous tactile happenings that occur in the watercolor and collage process can trigger a multitude of associations, leading you in different directions. Refer to pages 42–45 to recall how a representational subject evolved from the visual suggestions supplied by the developing painting itself. In this demonstration, the watercolor and collage process was also begun without a definite subject in mind. It was the developing painting that suggested the direction, and the work was completed according to this internal motivation. Try a similar process on your own, allowing yourself to be open to the visual suggestions of the developing work.

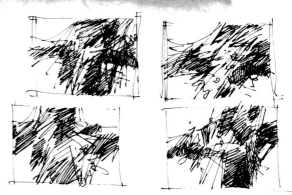

These quick concept sketches explore different compositional possibilities. All the concepts are workable, but the lower right one is selected as a basic design.

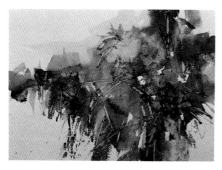

Watercolor in green-related hues is brushed directly on a sheet of 300 lb. rough paper. The overall shape is derived from the sketch. Scratches, spatters, and lifting with absorbent tissue provide the initial textural quality.

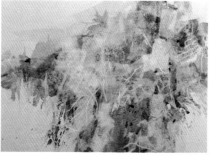

Pieces of torn Oriental papers are collaged to this surface, creating a layer of exciting textural variety. Note some color showing through the collage layer. No subject matter is anticipated at this point.

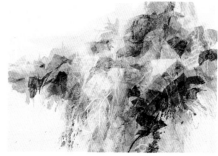

Watercolor washes are drybrushed onto the textured surface with a flat, ³/₄-inch sable brush. The light pattern is already becoming important in developing movement and passage on the surface.

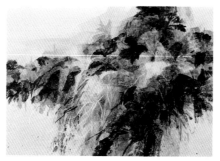

At this point the suggestion of rich foliage begins to exert itself. Because my recent work had dealt with Hawaiian subject matter, a Hawaiian hillside begins to emerge as the subject. This idea is clinched as more colors are applied.

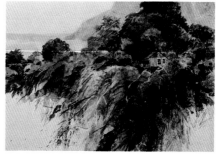

A typical Hawaiian cottage is placed in the area of emphasis, and visual movement is directed toward it. Trees, flowers, rocks, and the distant shoreline evolve from existing textures, suggested by the developing painting.

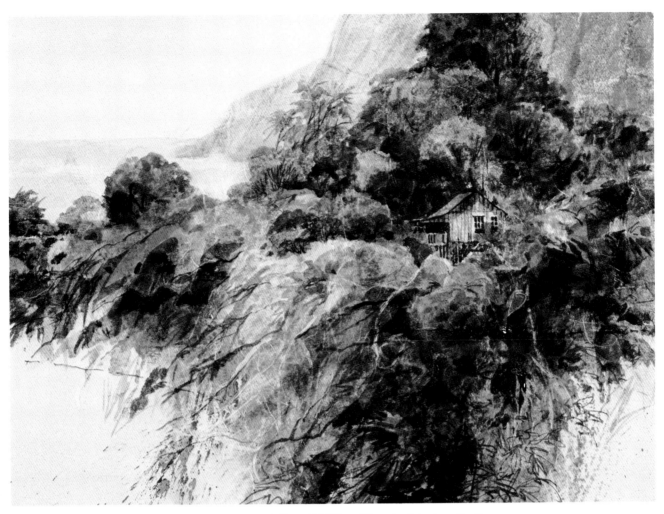

HAWAIIAN IMPRESSION. Watercolor and collage, 11" × 15" (28 × 38 cm). Private collection.

Once the commitment to subject matter has been made, several pieces of Oriental paper are added to emphasize the light-valued passage to the center of the painting. Other values are darkened and adjusted to suggest junglelike shadows. The cottage seems to nestle comfortably in an exotic jungle environment—an environment whose development depended totally on the internal motivation generated by the work itself.

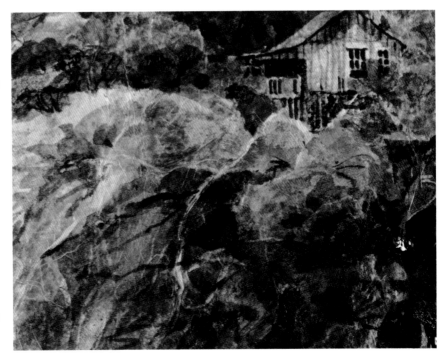

This detail reveals the complex layering process and the importance of line in the painting. The transparency of the watercolor medium is essential in taking advantage of the tactile quality of the collaged surface.

ADOPTING PROBLEM-SOLVING APPROACHES

Some artists like to pose problems or projects for themselves and use them as motivation for paintings. The focus may be on design, balance, contrast, visual dominance, shape, structure, movement, or any other painting problem. One artist may be challenged by balancing diverse aspects of a subject; another, by developing significant tension to make a painting exciting. Although at times such problems may seem to be simply mind-games, they can stimulate artists to approach a subject in new ways and thus produce exciting work.

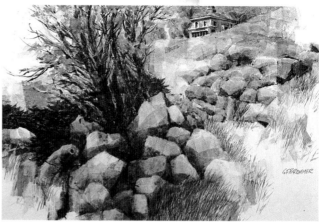

HIGH COUNTRY AUTUMN. Watercolor and collage, 15" × 22" (38 × 56 cm). Courtesy of Rosequist Galleries, Tucson, Arizona.

This painting grew out of a workshop experience, when part of a day was spent gathering visual information—in this case, sketching a variety of houses. The problem posed was to place a house at the top of the painting and design a suitable foreground in watercolor and collage, to support the structure. The solution involved several phases: (1) redrawing the house in proper perspective so it seemed far above the viewer's eye level; (2) designing an immediate environment for the house so it seemed comfortable atop the hill; and (3) designing the hillside to support the house and provide visual access (movement) to it. Obviously, this problem-solving project involved a great many of the tasks necessary to create any kind of painting.

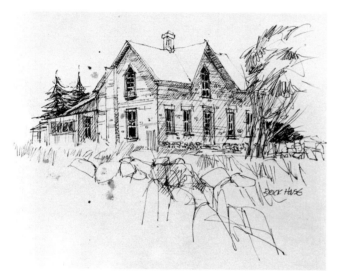

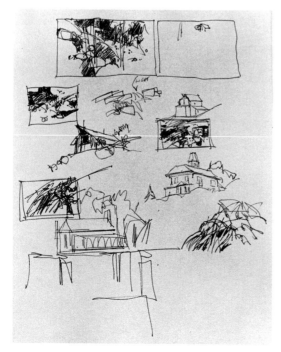

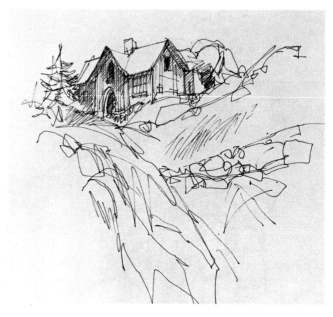

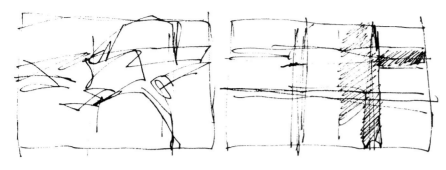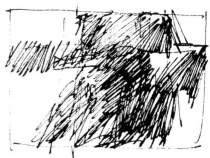

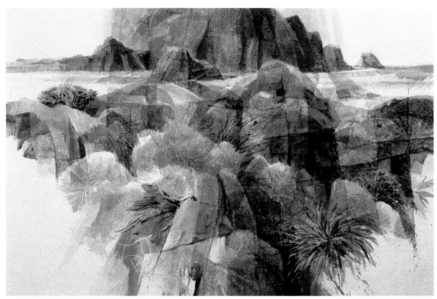

DESERT PATTERNS. Watercolor and collage, 15" × 22" (38 × 56 cm).
Courtesy of Rosequist Galleries, Tucson, Arizona.

Many artists choose their subjects first and then arrange the elements into suitable formats. An interesting alternative is to reverse the process: first establish a visual format (design) and then fit the subject matter to the established plan. Sketchbook doodles can often be the first step in developing such painting formats.

The two paintings shown here have obvious similarities in their formats, but they differ in their content. Both were begun as demonstration paintings, based on a single, small design sketch. The palette was purposely kept similar to emphasize the sameness in the developing paintings. Both looked very much alike after the first applications of watercolor and collage, but as the work continued, one came to represent a coastal location, the other a desert environment. No resource materials were used other than the paintings themselves and my memory and imagination.

Try filling several pages in your sketchbook with small design studies and then develop several paintings from one concept. By doing this, you will strengthen your own picture-making sense and learn to let the paintings themselves contribute to the construction of your finished work.

PACIFIC IMPRESSION. Watercolor and collage, 15" × 22" (38 × 56 cm).
Courtesy of Fireside Gallery, Carmel, California.

PERSONAL APPROACHES TO SOURCE MATERIAL

Just as there are many styles and techniques of painting, there are many ways to use source materials in developing concepts and ideas for painting. The artists whose work is shown on these two pages have found diverse ways to use the collaged papers themselves to generate paintings that are individual and personal. To develop your own personal expression, allow yourself to work with materials for the sheer joy of the process, rather than feeling you have to produce an exceptional product. Perhaps some of these personal approaches will provide ideas for your own explorations.

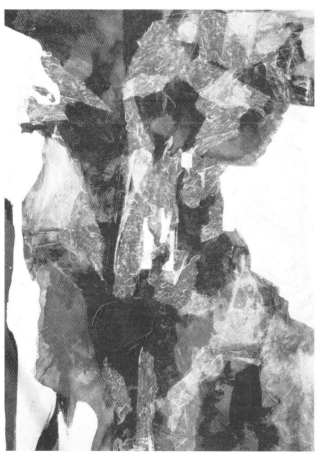

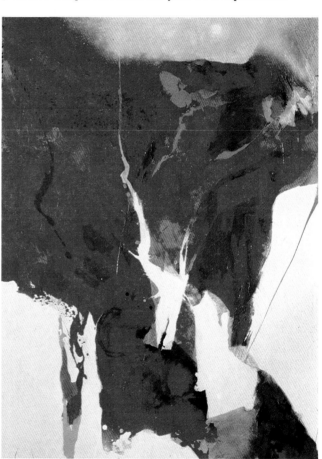

Edward Betts began this painting by collaging tissue papers and fibered Oriental papers to a gessoed Masonite panel and then painting them with red glazes (left). The idea was to explore shapes and textures and to establish a rich ground. After studying the resulting collage, he both brushed and sprayed acrylic paint to clarify the design concept. In his words, the configuration that developed "evoked cliff, ice, snow, and a hazy, wintry sun." Notice that the collage process is not very evident in the finished work. As Betts explains, "Collage served its purpose in stimulating ideas, but was then intentionally discarded or submerged in the finished state."

SNOW GORGE, by Edward Betts. Acrylic and collage on gessoed Masonite, 48" × 35" (122 × 89 cm). Private collection.

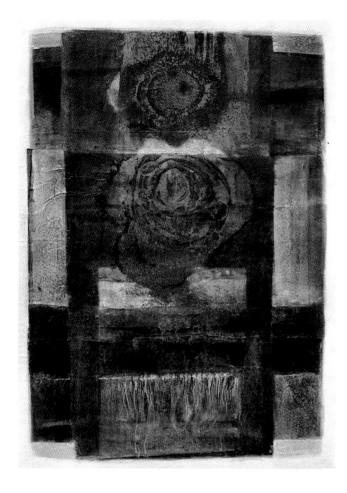

STONE SERIES 40, by Louise Cadillac. Watercolor, acrylic, and collage, 30" × 22" (76 × 56 cm). Private collection.

In Louise Cadillac's painting, alternating overlays of color and paper produce a fascinating textural surface, which almost simulates a woven fabric. The development of the collage itself dictates succeeding steps in this process, with the artist responding in a personal way. In some areas she uses line to emphasize the fabric-like quality, but generally she relies on shapes with various kinds of edges to create the subject.

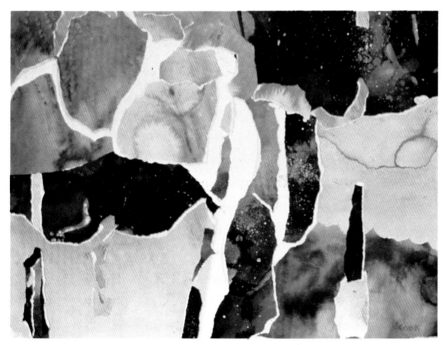

PATHS TO THE GALAXY III, by Jane Cook. Watercolor, acrylic, and collage, 14" × 19" (36 × 48 cm). Courtesy of the artist.

Jane Cook began this collage with an old painting, which she tore up and put back together to form a completely new statement. She used the torn painting fragments as shapes of value and color. Only after many trials in varying positions, however, did she decide on this grouping and collage the pieces in place. There is probably no relationship between this finished work and the original painting, other than color.

Try using your own paintings in similar ways to create a new generation of work. You can use the painting fragments as they are, or you might collage Oriental papers over them. You may wish to apply watercolor or other water media over either the collaged or uncollaged surface.

7
ALTERING UNSUCCESSFUL PAINTINGS

There are times when artists would like to make changes in their watercolor paintings. You might, for example, wish to change the path of visual movement in the foreground, or shift the center of interest to make the painting more interesting. Under normal circumstances, such changes are difficult to pull off with a transparent watercolor painting. Sometimes opaque water media can be introduced, but the unity of the surface can be difficult to maintain. Scrubbing and lifting color is an alternative, but if staining pigments have been used, there may be further problems.

Another solution is available, however—collaging Oriental papers on the surface and then completing the painting in transparent watercolor. This process allows the same medium and colors to be used, yet provides a way to cover the offending areas and prepare a new surface, ready for the unifying and finishing touches.

With collage, major surgery can be carried out at various times in the painting process. You can make alterations early in the painting process, when you first notice a need for improvement in structure or composition. The existing underpainting can be scrubbed out and redrawn and repainted, because the subsequent collaging will cover the scars of the original plan. You can also make changes while the collaged surface is being developed. The emphasis, direction, and composition can be altered, simply by restructuring the collage arrangement and finishing the painting in a different way. And after the painting is finished—even if it is signed, framed, and hanging—you can change it. Indeed, at any point, you can collage (or recollage) and repaint to effect the desired changes.

When collaging over a fully painted surface, try to apply the diluted glue or acrylic medium quickly and completely, without scrubbing the bristle brush on the sheet. If too many scrubbing strokes are made, the painted watercolor will dissolve in the glue and smear on the surface. This might not be objectionable in some cases, but a collaged surface is generally easier to design and manipulate if it is clean and dry.

It is possible to alter an entire sheet, thus designing a completely new image, or you may wish to change only a few square inches or centimeters. Whatever you decide to do, once you have experienced the ability to change and alter your watercolor paintings, you will gain confidence in trying out new ideas as you paint. Because you can always add collage, you need not be deeply concerned about making mistakes—a concern that unfortunately often leads to producing only "safe" paintings.

CHANGING A WATERCOLOR IN ITS EARLY STAGES

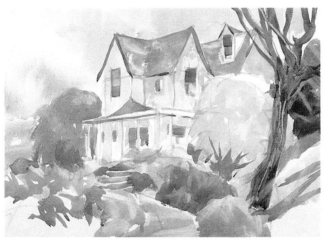

The subject of this watercolor is an old, abandoned house on the slope of Mingus Mountain in Jerome, Arizona. The initial painting illustrates the first step in the collage process: applying local color freely and quickly. The developing image, however, does not give the feeling of a house on a hillside, so changes will have to be made.

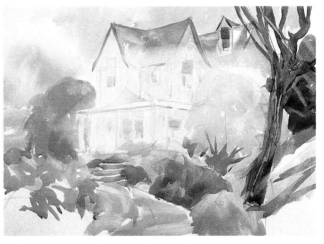

Before collaging, the central part of the surface is scrubbed briskly with a damp sponge and dried with absorbent tissue. Notice that Hookers Green Light, in particular, remains in some stained lines and shapes.

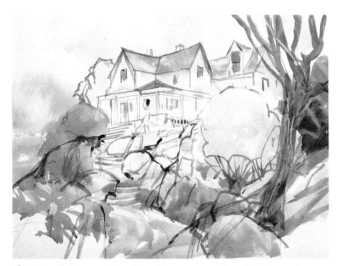

On top of the scrubbed surface, a new drawing is made, using watercolor and a pointed brush. The roof lines of the house are the same, but the house itself becomes smaller, allowing the foreground to be more fully developed and pushing the house further up. The hillside location of the house is now much more convincing.

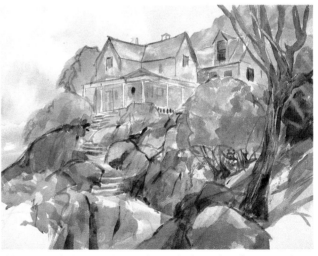

Watercolor is brushed onto the redesigned surface, much as in the initial painting step. When Oriental papers are added, this layer of color will not be completely visible, although it may show through in places. It is thus still possible to change the final form of the painting.

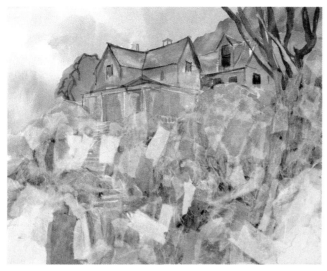

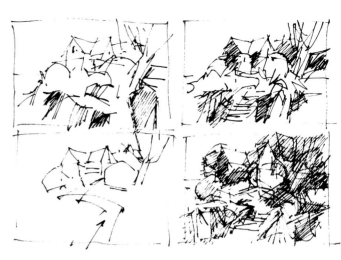

Torn pieces of many kinds of Oriental paper are collaged over the lower two-thirds of the surface. These papers are not torn to fit specific rock or foliage shapes, but are collaged at random.

Several thumbnail sketches suggest possible directions for the new composition. They need not be followed exactly, but they help fix a plan in mind that can set the brushes in motion.

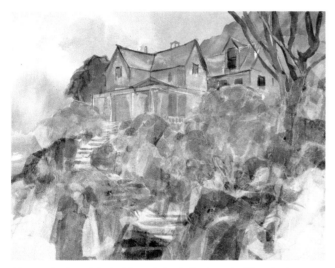

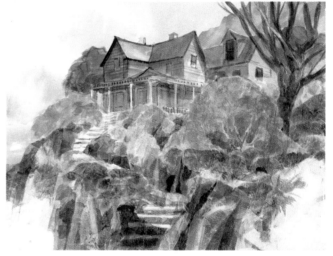

Now paint is added with a ³/₄-inch flat brush. The aim is to explore color and pattern on the dry, collaged surface. The house is not touched at this stage, nor are lines drawn on the hillside. Instead, the foreground is allowed to suggest its own development.

Gradually, visual movement and the basic forms on the hill are established. The house now receives some attention, to unify it with its environment.

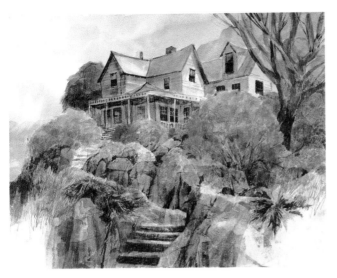

The house and hillside develop as a unit, and autumn warmth is suggested by the color and light. Details in the house, as well as cracks in the rocks, branches and twigs in the bushes and trees, and grass on the hillside, are added with a pointed brush. The whole painting moves toward a sharper focus.

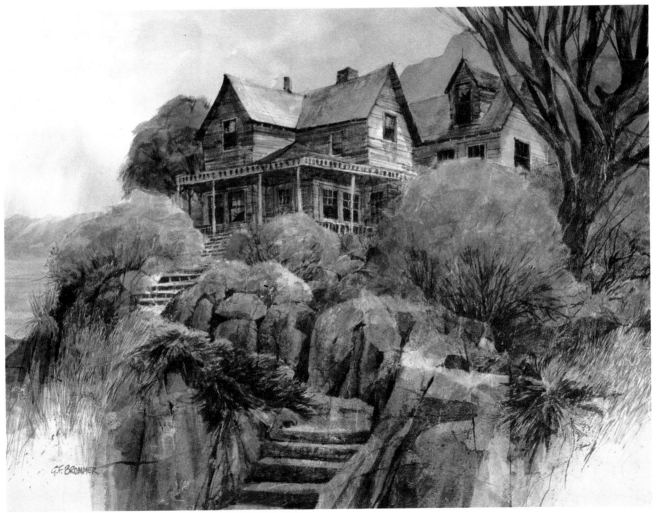

HOUSE IN JEROME. Watercolor and collage, 22" × 30" (56 × 78 cm). Collection of the artist.

The entire painting is gone over another time to fine-tune color and value relationships and to establish final detailing. Colors are lifted in a few places to clarify the light passage from the sky to the house. Middle values are also adjusted to weave the surface together. Through small adjustments in color, detail, and calligraphy, the work receives its identifying "signature" characteristics.

TRANSFORMING A FINISHED PAINTING

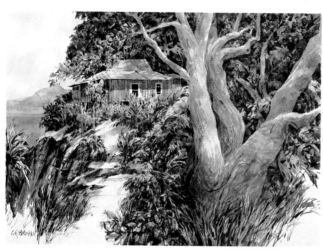

This watercolor painting of a hillside cottage on the island of Hawaii had been finished, signed, and framed. Indeed, it had already hung in several galleries. When the painting was returned to my studio, however, I felt that the visual emphasis was equally divided between the trees and the cottage; instead, one needed to be subordinated to the other. I decided to diminish the importance of the trees and enhance the visual dominance of the cottage.

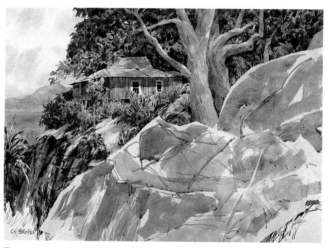

To help me visualize such a drastic change and its effect on the total composition, I tore several large pieces of bond paper and temporarily laid them over the lower part of the painting. After adding some neutral watercolor washes to kill the intense white, I could see how the composition might work. I decided to collage the foreground of the painting with Oriental papers, without any preliminary scrubbing of color.

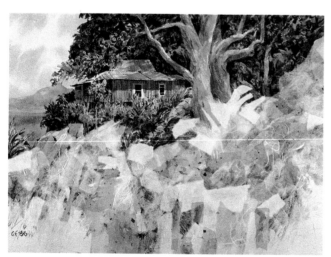

The next step was to select the Oriental papers. Because I wanted to create an impression of jungle rocks and undergrowth in the foreground, I chose the papers with these textures in mind. I also used some opaque white papers to drastically alter the existing value pattern. All these papers were applied directly to the painting, and the collaged surface was allowed to dry completely.

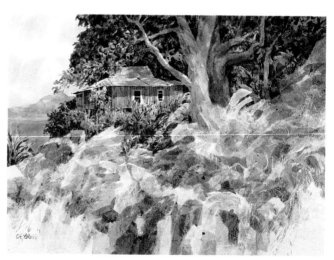

Using a 3/4-inch flat sable, I began brushing some foliage and rock colors over the dried collage. These were exploratory trials, made with my eyes squinted, to initiate appropriate light and dark patterns. I did not draw on the collaged surface, although that was an alternative.

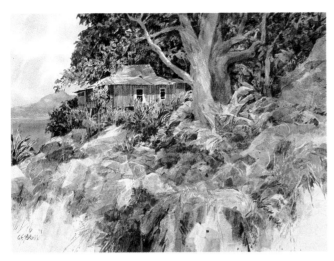

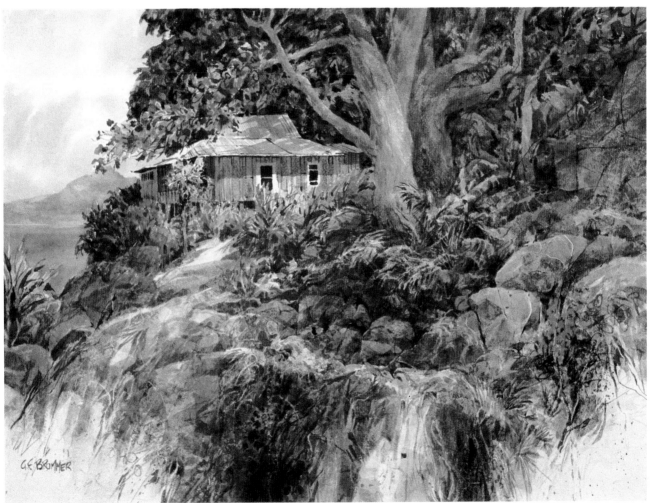

Working from memory and imagination, and stressing principles of composition (especially movement and balance), I added more color with both flat and pointed brushes. Notice that some of the calligraphic lines in the original painting are repeated in the newly collaged areas. Also observe how the dark values balance the painting and direct visual movement. At this point I still had a sense of exploration and trial, knowing that more paper could be collaged at any time.

BLUE HOUSE ON THE KONA COAST. Watercolor and collage, 22" × 30" (56 × 76 cm). Collection of Mr. and Mrs. Jack Fuhler.

In the finished painting, there is a clear visual movement to the center of interest—the house. Because the trees have been darkened in value and pushed into the shadows, the house stands out. The foreground is a bit out-of-focus as far as detail is concerned, but details come into focus near the center of interest. There is a transitional feeling of going from unfinished to finished areas, from negative to positive, from more abstract to more representational. The repetition of colors from the background in the foreground and the weaving of dark and light passages help to unify the whole.

ADDITIONAL BEFORE AND AFTER EXAMPLES

The three pairs of examples shown on these pages provide further insights into possible problems and solutions in altering existing watercolor paintings. One involves redesigning a finished collage painting; the other two show approaches to altering direct watercolors.

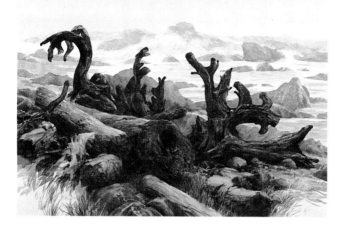

The clawlike driftwood logs along the Washington coast were the initial inspiration for this painting, and the stormy surf was relegated to a subordinate position. The finished watercolor was actually signed and delivered to a gallery for an exhibition. When the work was returned to the studio, however, it seemed overly dramatic and chaotic. By collaging Oriental papers in several places, I eliminated the most dramatic "claw" and changed the foreground. The final image still emphasizes the driftwood logs, but they are now part of a large, dark shape, which is more organized and less chaotic. The transition from foreground to middle ground is more gradual in the final version, and vertical edges are better defined, giving the painting more structure.

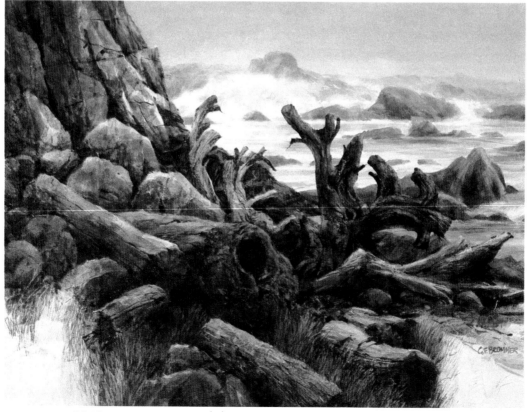

NORTHERN COAST. Watercolor and collage, 22" × 30" (56 × 76 cm). Private collection.

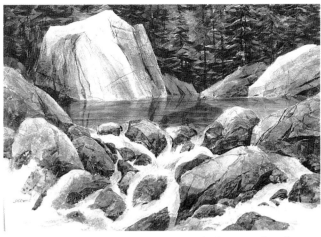

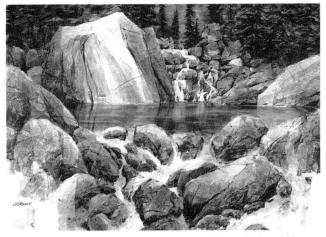

This painting has had three lives. Initially it was painted on location in Yosemite National Park and finished as a direct watercolor. Later, in the studio, the rocks and rushing water were collaged with Oriental papers and repainted, as seen here in the before condition. But the pattern of rocks and water in the foreground seemed uninteresting, and there was no evident source for the water supply. The solution involved collaging over the trees in the middle ground and designing a tumbling cascade, which both provided a water source and visually tied the foreground to the middle ground. The foreground cascade was also recollaged and repainted.

HIGH SIERRA POOL. Watercolor and collage, 22″ × 30″ (56 × 76 cm). Courtesy of Louis Newman Galleries, Beverly Hills, California.

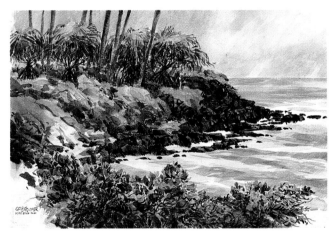

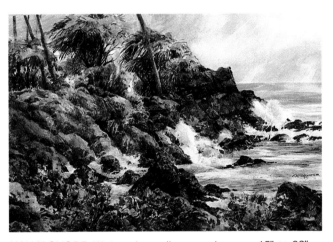

This painting of the rocky, lava shore at Poipu Beach in Hawaii began its life as a demonstration watercolor, painted on location during a workshop. The emphasis was on the local color and foliage. Then, during a studio workshop where collage techniques were being demonstrated, the entire concept was changed to feature the rocky shore during a surging tropical storm. By adding collage and white gesso, I altered the entire surface, except for part of the sky. Cliffs, trees, surf, and foliage were all redesigned to meet the visual requirements of a storm.

KAUAI SHORE. Watercolor, collage, and gesso, 15″ × 22″ (38 × 56 cm). Private collection

8
LEARNING FROM COLLAGE

Collage artists work primarily with paper in various ways, gluing pieces to surfaces to create their work. Some add painting or drawing to their visual statements, while others use only papers. Some prepare their papers by staining, silkscreening, or painting them; others use only found papers in their work. Some emphasize texture; others specialize in color and shape. The variety of techniques and approaches to using collage alone is formidable and exciting.

But you do not have to work primarily in collage to benefit from the collage experience. Combining collage with various water media can open a completely new set of doors to inquiring artists. Because the collage process invites experimentation, it can lead to new directions in your painting, whatever your preferred medium is. Although the emphasis in this chapter is on the combination of collage and transparent watercolor, the comments about constructing successful paintings apply to all media. Through working with collage, you should be able to communicate more effectively in your chosen medium.

Any new visual experience tends to increase awareness. Working with collage can sharpen perceptions and stimulate ideas. In particular, collage generates a greater awareness of texture and its importance in designing effective paintings.

You will probably find yourself noticing textures more in your immediate environment, and you may begin to use a greater variety of simulated textures in direct watercolor paintings.

Another benefit of the watercolor and collage process is that it relies on instant reactions to unpredictable events that take place on the textured surface. By learning to respond to developing situations in the collage process, you will become more creative in solving problems as they arise in any painting. You may tend to look more to the work itself for ideas and directions as your painting progresses. Moreover, your desire and ability to experiment with any painting medium should increase. And it is through experimentation that we grow as artists and add new dimensions to our expressive capabilities.

Yet another advantage of exploring collage is that it can heighten your awareness of the importance of design in constructing a painting. With collage, you can manipulate the surface and rearrange the visual elements into the most effective composition. This ability to redesign the surface of paintings allows you to come to grips with the essentials of good composition. Then, when you make preliminary sketches, you should be able to anticipate and eliminate many problem situations.

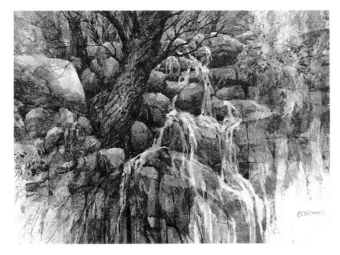

AFTER AN AUTUMN RAIN. Watercolor and collage, 15″ × 22″ (38 × 56 cm). Collection of Len Brugano.

Working with collage can increase your awareness of texture and its use in painting. The subject of After an Autumn Rain *is an imaginary scene, which evolved from the collage process itself. It was the rich, tactile surface created by the collaged Oriental papers that suggested the subject matter of rocks, trees, and water. In the finished painting, the passage of light holds the textures in place, but the tapestry-like surface remains the dominant aspect. A few nontextured areas allow the viewer's eyes to rest a bit, but they are quickly drawn back into the textural spaces.*

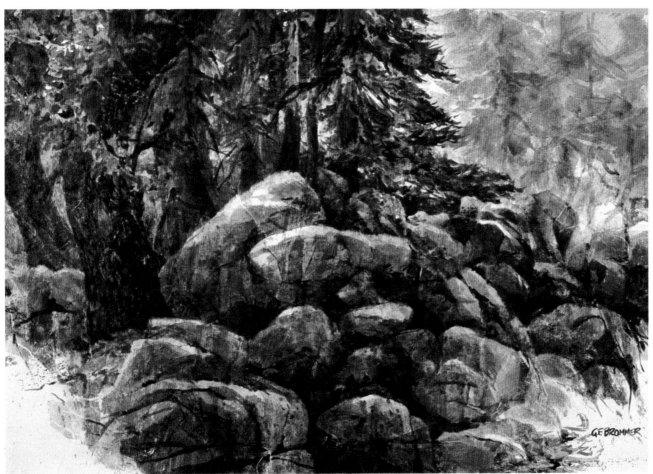

RAINY LIGHT. Watercolor and collage, 15″ × 22″ (38 × 56 cm). Collection of Pacific Telesis Group, San Francisco, California.

This piece was done as a workshop demonstration. Its subject was derived partly from a rainy scene outside the studio window and partly from the suggestions supplied by the developing painting. Textures dominate the surface, which was purposely kept low-keyed to convey rainy light during a mountain thunderstorm. Notice how visual movement is maintained even in such a chaotic environment.

BROADENING YOUR STYLE AND WORKING TECHNIQUES

Working with collage will affect your personal style of communication. Indeed, every visual experience affects your style to some degree. And the more you allow yourself to experiment and grow, the more your style will become specifically personal. Many artists have developed unique styles in making their collage statements, and have then adapted these styles to direct watercolor painting or other water media techniques.

Because you can always rework the painting surface, collage encourages you to experiment and make changes in your working methods. This can add flair to your style and make you less inhibited in your approach to painting. Paintings need not be precious, but can be constructed and altered to produce dynamic visual statements.

Working with collage not only gives you the opportunity to make different kinds of statements and develop new styles of presentation; it also provides you with a completely new set of techniques. At times, you may feel frustrated at not being able to say what you wish to say with your usual techniques. Perhaps collage can help you make a more definitive visual statement. Or you may be tired of working in the same way

every day, day after day. Perhaps by combining collage and watercolor, the creative juices will begin to flow again. Often a change in working methods can provide the impetus for new and exciting images.

Working with watercolor and collage can also lead to new insights into the entire painting process. It may, for instance, provide an entry into the world of abstraction, by involving you directly with abstract approaches to picture making. Even if you are not an abstract artist, this experience can be helpful in fostering an understanding of the total world of artistic expression. Remember that the same principles of composition underlie all good painting, whether it is realistic or abstract. If you increase your understanding of these principles, you will be better able to make effective visual statements.

In general, when you allow yourself to work in alternative techniques, styles, and materials, you provide yourself with a broader range of expression. The more options you have as an artist, the sharper you become in choosing the most adequate ways to communicate your ideas and feelings through your art.

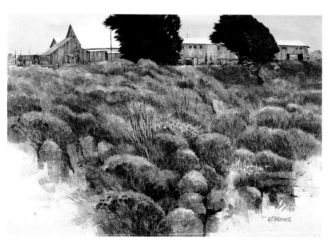

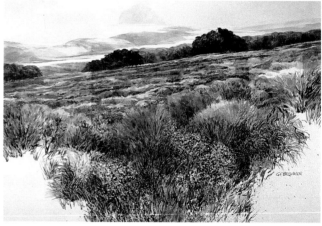

COASTAL RANCH/NORTH OF SANTA CRUZ. Watercolor and collage; 22" × 30" (56 × 76 cm). Collection of Pacific Telesis Group, San Francisco, California.

THE COAST AT MORRO BAY. Watercolor, 22" × 30" (56 × 76 cm). Courtesy of Fireside Gallery, Carmel, California.

Artists should allow different working experiences to influence the technique, colors, moods, and compositional characteristics of subsequent paintings. Here the watercolor and collage painting on the left had a definite influence on the watercolor painting done several years later. Both use the same basic design concept, with a high horizon and receding space. Also notice that in both the richly textured foreground gives way to less textured deep space. Although, in the background, the fog-shrouded rock differs from the long barn and trees, they have a similar importance in the two works.

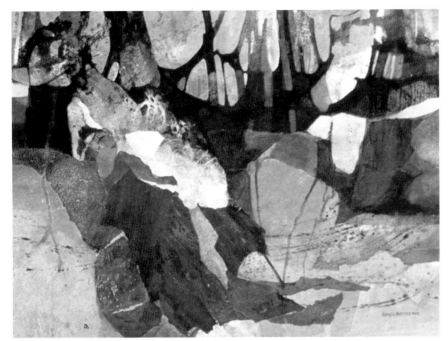

A FOREST PLACE, by Carole Barnes.
Acrylic and collage, 22" × 30"
(56 × 76 cm). Private collection.

Many of Carole Barnes's paintings deal with abstracted landscape elements, and this pair is no exception. The shapes, colors, textures, and strong design that characterize her collage paintings also typify her acrylics. But it was collage that originally generated the strengths found in her current acrylic paintings. She says, "I have always used collage to pull me back into strong color contrasts when I felt my paint choices were becoming timid. Realizing the sameness of shape in collage and painted pieces . . . helps me paint with surer intent." Collage need not tear you away from your current techniques or style, but it can augment and strengthen your painting methods, and allow you to communicate more forcefully.

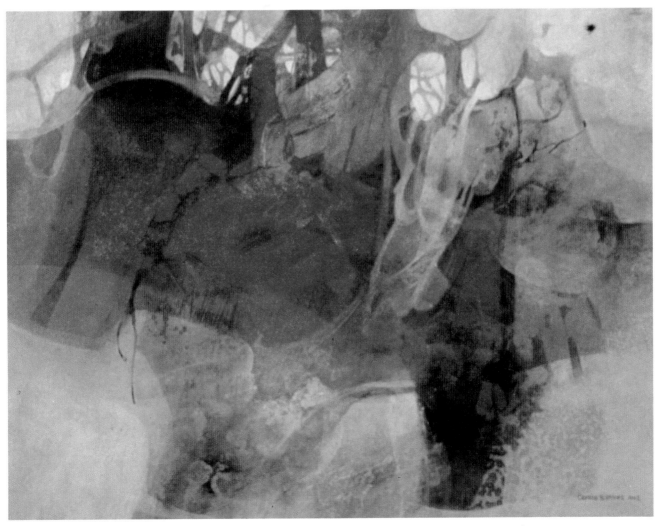

SYMPHONY OF A LANDSCAPE, by Carole Barnes. Acrylic, 21" × 27" (53 × 69 cm). Private collection.

NURTURING AN EXPERIMENTAL ATTITUDE

Working with collage is a sure-fire way to develop and nurture an experimental attitude toward painting techniques and design. The first time you tear a piece of paper, you sense that you are working with an unpredictable shape—and this fosters a desire to experiment further to bring it under control. This experimental attitude, born in and nurtured with collage experiences, can carry over into other media, such as direct watercolor painting. As the examples on this spread and the next illustrate, experimenting with collage can lead to the discovery of new design formats and an expanded artistic vocabulary. Remember that the more chances you take, the more you are willing to experiment and to stretch the limits of your aesthetic understanding, the more you will grow as an artist.

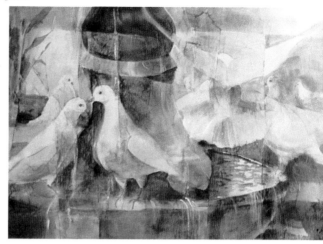

FOUNTAIN FRIENDS, by Helen B. Reed. Watercolor, acrylic, and collage, 18" × 24" (46 × 61 cm). Collection of Mr. and Mrs. George Niles.

Helen Reed's experimental approach is evident in both of these examples, but what is even more striking is how her water-media painting takes on the appearance of a collage, even though no papers have been added. Vertical and horizontal lines and the development of transparent, overlapping planes have become identifying characteristics of Reed's work. After planning her composition in a sketchbook, she works the surface carefully to arrive at the appearance of overlapping planes. She experiments by spattering rubbing alcohol on acrylics to produce textures and by scratching lines in watercolor with brush handles. At times she may add a veil of thinned white acrylic over transparent watercolor washes, or she may mix gloss and matte mediums. She is constantly exploring new methods of working with materials, as well as unique ways to organize her surfaces.

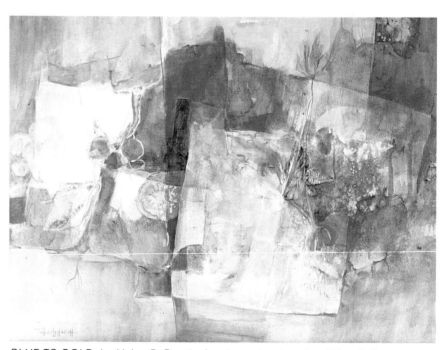

BLUE TO GOLD, by Helen B. Reed. Acrylic and watercolor, 18" × 24" (46 × 61 cm). Private collection.

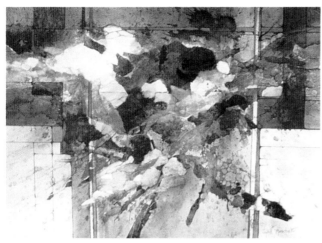

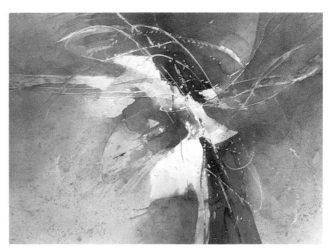

ROCKY HILLSIDE, by Sybil Moschetti. Watercolor, acrylic, pencil, and collage on 300 lb. cold-pressed paper, 22" × 30" (56 × 76 cm). Collection of Pratt Community College, Pratt, Kansas.

SWING THAT LARIAT, by Sybil Moschetti. Watercolor, 30" × 45" (76 × 114 cm.) Collection of Dr. and Mrs. G. T. Anderson.

Sybil Moschetti's experimental attitude is reflected in both her collages and her watercolor paintings. Rocky Hillside began when Moschetti tore up some unsuccessful watercolors and glued them to a sheet of 300 lb. cold-pressed paper. She added Oriental papers to soften edges and provide transitional passages and used pencil to define the rocklike forms and other shapes. The composition, however, did not seem satisfactory, so she placed pieces of tape in vertical and horizontal configurations and added more color and line. When the tape was removed, it left crisp edges, which contrasted nicely with the soft edges of the papers. After some final color touches, the work was finished.

In Swing That Lariat, Moschetti was just as experimental as she was with the collage. After taping freezer paper to the surface to protect white spaces, she added lines of Luma masking liquid, using different-size squeeze bottles. Allowing for drying time between each phase, she introduced stains, lines, and washes in ever-darkening values. When the masks were removed, she added lines to connect the visual movement. She also dropped salt in a few wet areas. After pausing to critique the design, Moschetti lifted some areas of color and added some darker values. She also used a hypodermic needle to suck up color and squirt it onto the surface, before she made her final adjustments.

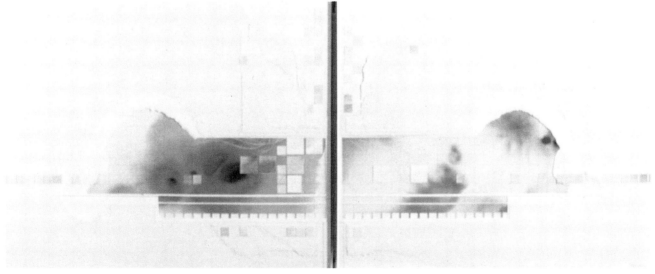

TUCSON, AFTER THE RAINS: BEFORE THE RUSH, by Nanci Blair Closson. Watercolor and layered rag mat diptych, 32" × 80" overall (81 × 204 cm). Private collection.

Nanci Closson has worked with collage for many years, and this image is an extension of her experiments with the medium. She started with an abstract watercolor painting, over which she applied several layers of torn and cut rag matboards to produce a sculptural surface. At times she used the off-white matboard as it was manufactured, or she might dip and paint pieces to vary them slightly from each other. After building the surface, she introduced pencil lines and collaged additional pieces of cut-out watercolor paper and matboard; she then added watercolor as needed. Although made of watercolor and paper, the collage is actually a low-relief construction.

INSIDE/OUTSIDE, by Guenther Riess. Watercolor, acrylic, and paper construction, 30" × 36" (76 × 91 cm). Private collection.

The painted constructions of Guenther Riess are architectonic in nature and far different in character from most of the landscape collages included in this book. Riess uses themes found outside his studio windows in New York City to trigger his imagination. In this diptych-like presentation, we look into his studio window on the left side and out of his studio window on the right. Using rag papers, matboard, and gesso, Reiss constructed the architectural elements and three-dimensional studio furniture. He then set up an exciting visual tension by painting illusionistic details in watercolor and acrylic. Certainly, this is a unique, personal approach to collage and water media.

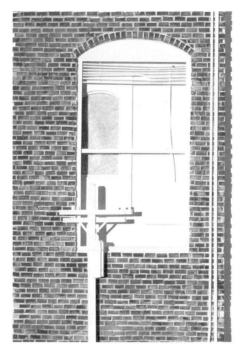
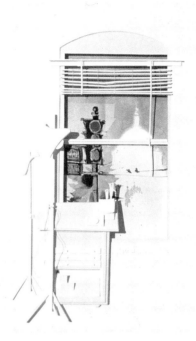

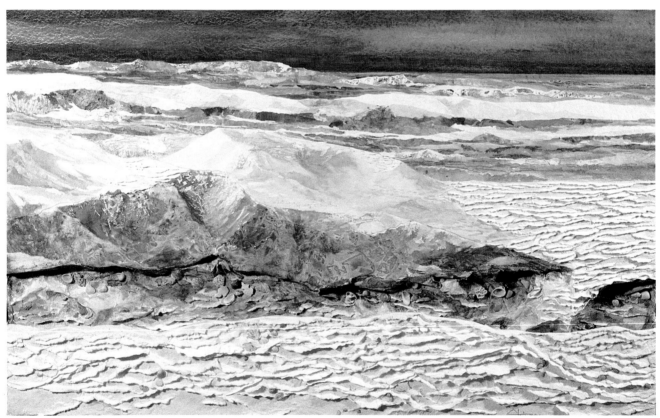

BACK DUNES, by Chispa Bluntzer. Watercolor, Prismacolor, sea shells, and collage, 24" × 40" × 1¹/₂" (46 × 102 × 4 cm). Private collection.

Chispa Bluntzer wanted to go beyond a textural surface, so she devised ways to "build" her paintings in several layers, using handmade and watercolor papers as well as small objects like sea shells. She explains, "I like to allow the viewer to peek into the crevices, be it of dunes, or of cliffs and creeks." In this work, the sand ripples and rock ledges are raised and emphasize the sculptural quality of her subject.

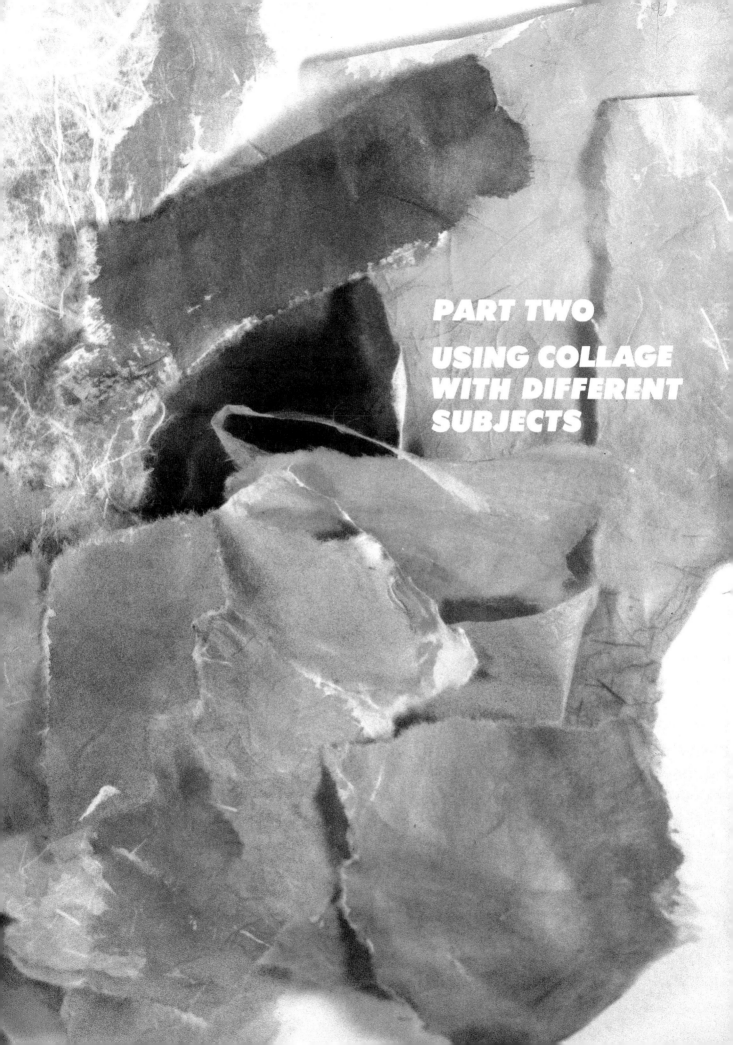

PART TWO

USING COLLAGE
WITH DIFFERENT
SUBJECTS

9 ROCKS

Many painters complain of difficulty in placing convincing rocks in their paintings. Although the textures of some Oriental papers can suggest rocklike textures, you must still observe various kinds of rocks and draw and paint them to become familiar with their forms and surface characteristics. Gather a handful of rocks and put them on a table in your studio; look at them and draw them. Put a strong light on them to see how shadows and highlights can be used to make them look convincingly three-dimensional. Remember that rocks are heavy, so your depiction of them should indicate weight and mass.

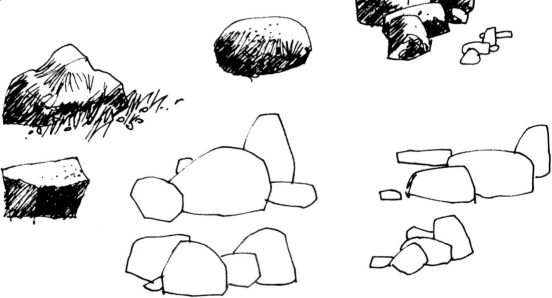

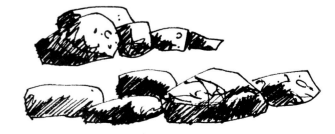

Sketch a cluster of rocks, first in contour and then with shading. Use hard-edged shadows to indicate crisp, sharp edges and gradual shading to suggest rounded forms. Note how the rock shapes overlap each other and what happens to the bottoms of rocks that rest on the ground. If you look down on rocks, the bottoms are usually rounded. Only if you are looking straight at them do the bottoms appear flat. Softening the bottom edge will create the feeling that rocks are resting in grass, not on top of it.

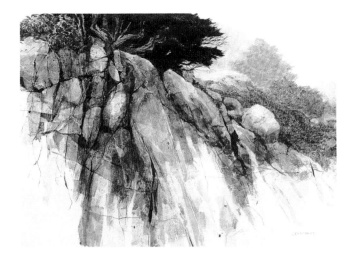

ROCKS, FOG AND TREES/CARMEL HARMONY. Watercolor and collage, 22″ × 30″ (56 × 76 cm). Collection of Charles Lamar.

This is an imaginary subject, painted to emphasize the rocky cliffs, softened by the fog. The high horizon and diagonal composition create a strong upward thrust that focuses attention on the austere power of the rocks. The rock forms are built from pieces of heavy, 300 lb. rough and cold-pressed paper, as well as a variety of Oriental papers. The spaces between the heavy papers suggest the deep crevices between rocks. The cool, dark shadows in these crevices contrast sharply with the sun-drenched cliffside. The soft, fog-shrouded foliage then acts as a foil for the crisp, hard-edged rocks. Note the variety of lines and how some are determined by the collage, while others unite parts of the surface.

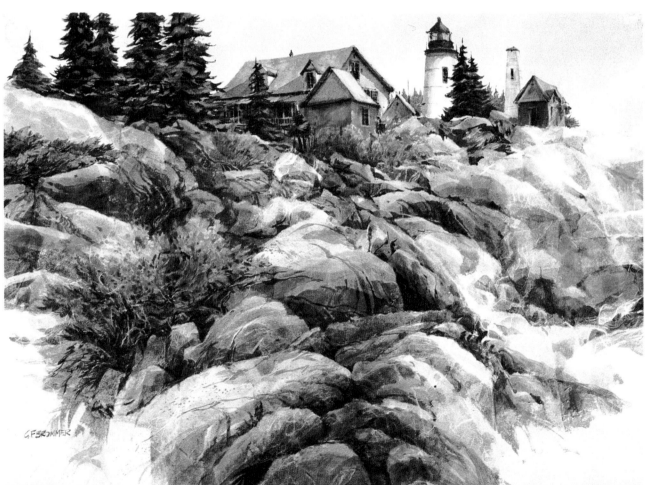

PEMAQUID. Watercolor and collage, 22″ × 30″ (56 × 76 cm). Collection of John Frazier.

Although these rocks were painted to suggest the rocks of the Pemaquid area in Maine, they are not exactly like them. Care was taken to provide visual movement in the form of light passage from the bottom corners upward into the painting, terminating at the cluster of buildings atop the rocky hill. Notice how the cool, autumn light is reflected off the damp rock faces and glares white, while the shadows remain deep and cool. The rocks are painted in a variety of local colors, from white to black and many shades of brown. Some have crisp edges and others are rounded and worn; some have contour lines to indicate mass and others do not, relying only on changes in value. The soft foliage is important in itself, but also helps make the rocks seem harder and heavier. The color on the right is mostly the first application of watercolor showing through the collaged papers.

DEPICTING ROCKS IN STREAMS

It can be enjoyable to paint rocks in a mountain stream, where both the rocks and rushing water have characteristic textures. The first basic decision that you must make, however, is what to emphasize. Do you want the viewer to focus on the rocks or on the water? Although both subjects can be important, one should dominate.

Your sources of information can range from starts made on location to slides and photographs; from sketches to your imagination. Keep in mind that rocks in different parts of the world have different colors, textures, forms, and geological sources. Study them carefully; then make your own generalizations as you draw and paint. Make several sketches to position the clusters and individual rocks, and watch for typical shadows, highlights, and middle values. All of this information is essential once you begin to work and translate your impressions and feelings of the rocks and stream into a visual form. Simplify your sketches and the layout for the painting; then develop the necessary specifics as you work on your painting and collage.

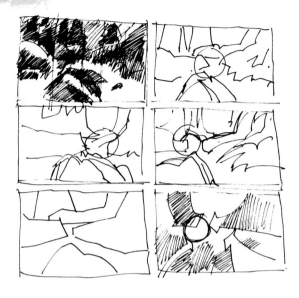

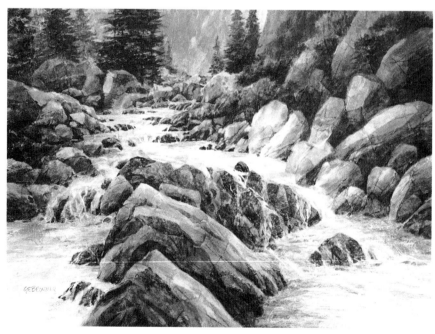

HIGH COUNTRY STREAM. Watercolor and collage, 15" × 22" (38 × 56 cm). Collection of Mr. and Mrs. Jack Bowman.

These sketches show how to simplify and isolate the basic elements in a scene. Explore several trial arrangements, moving the basic shapes into different positions. Once your linear composition is established, a value sketch can help to locate the main dark, medium, and light areas, suggesting passage and visual movement. Only after you have done this kind of preparatory visual probing are you ready to start painting.

My first step here was to draw and quickly paint the subject and then collage the entire surface with Oriental papers. Next, the basic rock formations were laid down in light values over the textured surface. The shapes of individual rocks began to exert themselves. They were not necessarily the same as the rocks in nature, but the painting became more important than nature at this point. Indeed, I abandoned my source material (a colored slide) and developed the rocks according to the textural suggestions of the papers themselves. The painting took on its own light source and visual identity.

In the finished painting, the sizes and colors of rocks vary as does the textural treatment. Some are in bright light, others in deep shadow. Note the passage from white water into the light-value faces of some rocks.

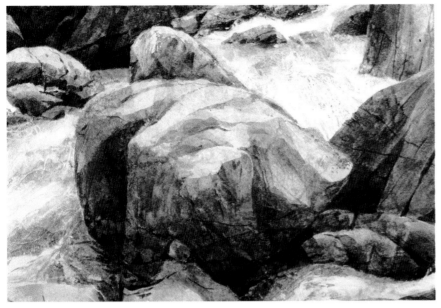

This detail of another painting (see the full reproduction on page 68) reveals the incredible textural complexity that you can achieve with collaged papers and watercolor. The surface configuration of the boulder in front was developed primarily with a wide, dry brush. Details were added with a pointed sable. Notice the range of values, from very light to very dark.

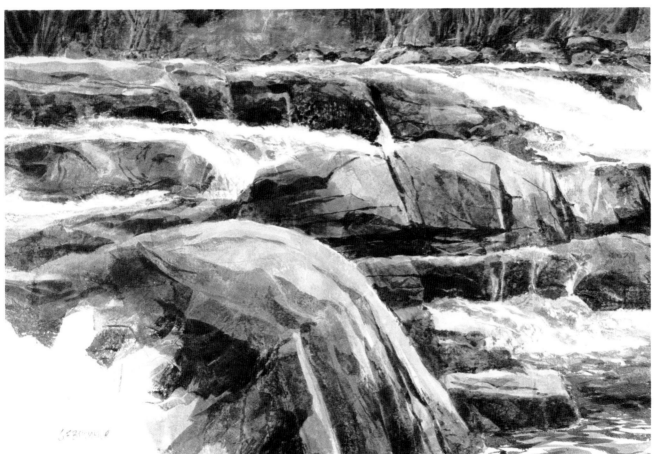

VERMONT STREAM/AUTUMN. Watercolor and collage, 15" × 22" (38 × 56 cm). Collection of Jan Moorman.

Dramatic granite shelves and boulders are featured in this Vermont scene. A slight indication of fall foliage is suggested at the top of the high-horizon format. Essentially the painting consists of a series of horizontal wedges, tied together vertically by value shifts and tumbling water. The passage of light, moving easily from the rocks to the water in places, visually welds the disparate elements together. Sharp shadows then heighten the feeling of crisp edges.

After the initial painting was brushed on quickly and the entire half-sheet was collaged with Oriental papers, most of the subsequent painting was done with a 3/4-inch flat brush, to emphasize the large shapes of the rocky shelves. A pointed brush was used to detail local texture and to echo the horizontal movement and vertical fracturing established in the rock shapes. Very little color was added in the water areas, to maintain the visual sensation of a tumbling stream.

MAKING ROCKS PART OF THE ENVIRONMENT

Rocks can be the dominant element in a painting, but they can also be a subordinate part of an environment featuring other elements. The three examples on these pages were painted from sketchbook drawings, done in various parts of the world. In one, rocks are incidental to the subject; in another, they have been cut and modified by humans; and in the third, they are the dominant natural element and occupy most of the pictorial space.

Although three completely different types of rocks are represented here, all are painted with the same basic watercolor and collage techniques, and they share a concern with shape, form, texture, and line. Specifically, all were first drawn as shapes with pencil on the textured ground. Then, when colors were added, the textures of the Oriental papers were emphasized and the colors suggested form and dimension. As the paintings developed, line was introduced to sharpen edges, emphasize crevices, establish contours, and create additional texture.

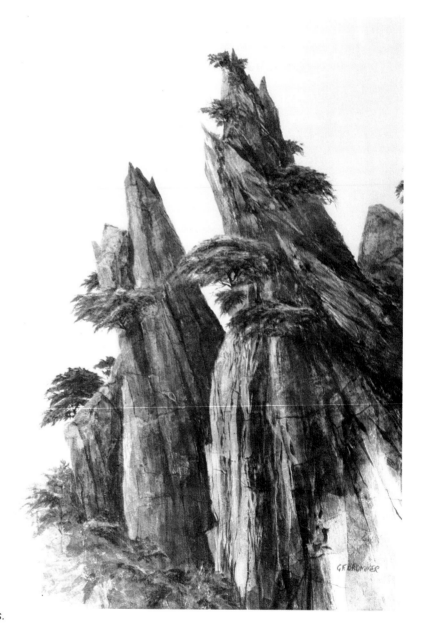

SILENT MOUNTAIN/CHINA. Watercolor and collage, 30" × 22" (76 × 56 cm). Private collection.

These jagged protrusions are clearly isolated from their environment and treated as featured stars in a visual production. The trees have a slightly softening effect and provide some environmental interest, but the contrast of the thrusting rocks against the gentle sky emphasizes their hardness and crisp texture. Observe the use of value and line to bring out the overall dramatic form, sharp edges, and textural details. In general, the painting is handled like a portrait, with the focus on the distinctive characteristics of the rocks.

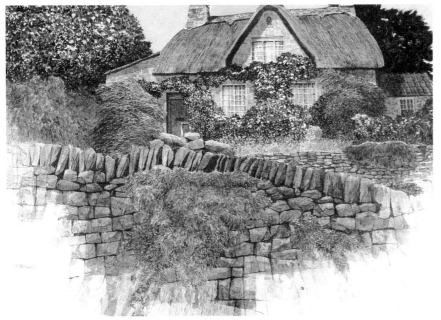

CASTLE COMBE FARMHOUSE. Watercolor and collage on cold-pressed paper, 22" × 30" (56 × 76 cm). Collection of Thomas Kemp.

The subject of this painting is a farmhouse, originally sketched in the English Cotswolds. As the painting developed, the cut and stacked stones in the foreground wall became important elements in creating a sense of space. Notice how the individual stones have been delineated to emphasize their hand-hewn, geometric quality. The spaces between these stones are very dark because no light reaches into the deep crevices. The various kinds of foliage act as foils, softening the surface and adding emphasis to the crisp stone shapes. The foliage also serves as a bridge from the lower part of the painting, which is collaged, to the upper part, which is not.

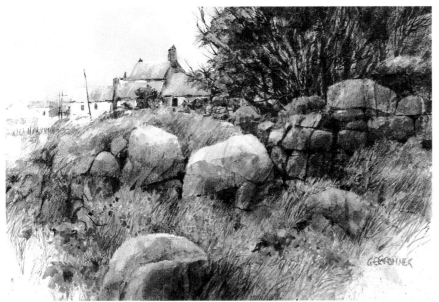

IRISH SPRING. Watercolor and collage, 15" × 22" (38 × 56 cm).
Collection of Mr. and Mrs. Stan Pratt.

This collage began with an abstract sketch, similar to the ones illustrated in Chapter 1. Only as additional color was brushed on the collage surface did the subject suggest itself. At this point the cluster of Irish houses was chosen from a sketchbook and drawn on the surface with a pencil. The trees, grass, flowers, and rocks derived from the developing painting, not the original sketch.

Overlapping elements and visual passage weave the surface of the finished work together. Line is used to emphasize the crevices in and between rocks, and also to suggest grass and the thicket branches. Notice the way the grass overlaps the bottoms of the rocks to create the appearance of rocks resting in the grass. Spots of color suggest flowers, but they are not painted in detail because they are incidental to the dominant subject.

CREATING AN IMPRESSION OF ROCKY CLIFFS

Few places on earth can match Pemaquid Point in Maine for its incredibly textured rocks and cliffs. The textural quality of this environment is so complex that it would be difficult to capture the multitude of intricate swirls, caverns, striations, and twists in the rocky promontory. Instead, I have attempted to capture an impression of the place—a glimpse of the twisted contours of a magical site.

After a few sketches on scratch paper, an outline is drawn with a pointed brush, in a neutral hue.

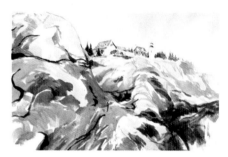

The surface is quickly covered with light values of local colors. Crevices are indicated with dark lines. The light values already suggest passage and visual movement.

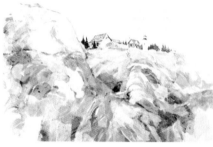

With the exception of the soft sky and most of the buildings, everything is covered with torn pieces of several kinds of Oriental paper.

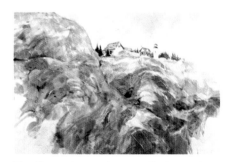

The first color washes applied over the collaged surface are warm earthtones. A few areas are left unpainted.

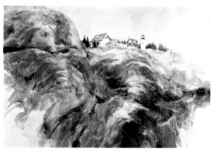

Cool grays are brushed over the warm earthtones in places to indicate shadows and form. A few dark areas infer deep shadows. The papers begin to suggest textural richness.

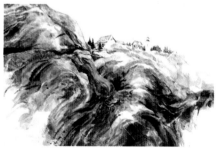

Although local textures and striations are derived from the sketchbook notes and slides of the area, the individual characteristics of the collaged papers are still emphasized. Note the increasing involvement with the rocks and the decreasing importance of the structures.

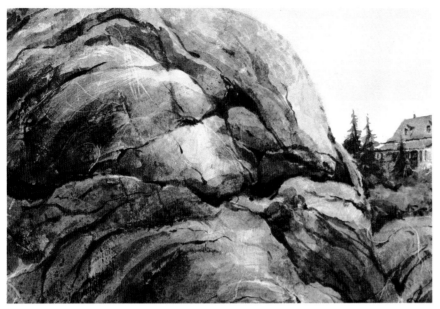

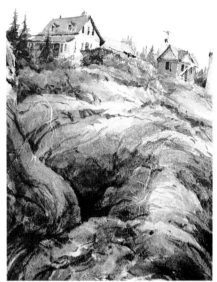

This detail shows the use of line and very dark shapes to simulate deep crevices in the rocky surface. But you also need a complete range of values to make the rocky forms convincingly dimensional, solid, and massive. Note how both painted textures and the papers' textures are used to portray the complex surface.

Remember to tie collaged and uncollaged areas together in style and technique. Here the buildings are not collaged, yet they are completely integrated with the collaged surface. Your handling of values and of the medium itself can help to unify the painting surface.

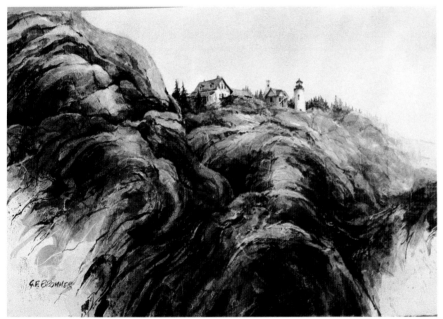

PEMAQUID IMPRESSION. Watercolor and collage, 15" × 22" (38 × 56 cm). Collection of Mr. and Mrs. David Walther.

Although I could have stopped the painting at several junctures along the way, I decided to carry the texturing process to this point, to emphasize the incredibly complex surface—a geologist's dream. On the right, the various Oriental papers suggest a foggy atmosphere, in contrast to the central core and left side, which are completely painted and fully articulated. Both dark and light passages direct the eye through the work to the lighthouse structures, but it is the rocky surface that remains the dominant feature of the painting.

PERSONAL APPROACHES TO ROCKS

Each artist develops personal approaches to all types of subject matter, even rocks. Indeed, rocks can become the special realm of an artist's visual activity. Alexander Nepote, for example, has spent a great deal of time exploring ways to work with cliffs and rocks, and has developed an exciting, distinctive style as a result of this concentration. The other artists whose work is shown here have also developed individual responses to rocks. Their varied techniques may inspire you to explore this subject matter further on your own.

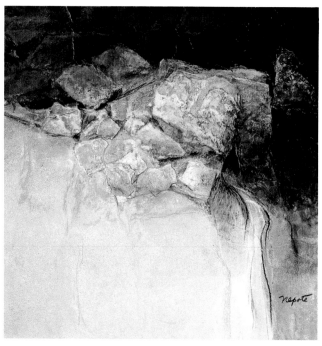

CLIFF CASCADE, by Alexander Nepote. Watercolor and collage on watercolor board, 14" × 14" (36 × 36 cm). Collection of the artist.

Many of Alexander Nepote's pieces are huge in size, but even this small image has monumental qualities. His aim is to represent "cliffness" in his work, and he uses collage techniques to accomplish this goal. Papers are glued, painted, and sanded, recollaged, and reworked on a watercolor board surface; color is lifted, added, scrubbed off, and added again. Any and every process is important in developing the complex, textured surface. As Nepote explains, "The actual physical technique of building a composition by adding layers, some on top of each other, some adjacent, some overlapping, and working into these layers by cutting, peeling off, scrubbing, etc., makes it possible for me to develop my concepts into meaningful paintings." He often works from sketches, but once the process starts it becomes self-motivating, and he enjoys the challenge of unpredictability and of fusing the predictable and unpredictable into a unified whole. As a final touch, he may add accents with pastel or conté crayon to spark the surface to life.

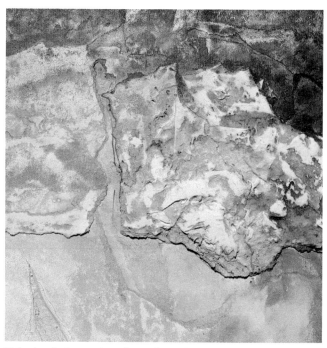

This detail shows the effect of carefully sanding the surface to lift color and reintroduce white. The process takes advantage of the rough-textured surface of watercolor paper and adds to the complexity of the layered textures.

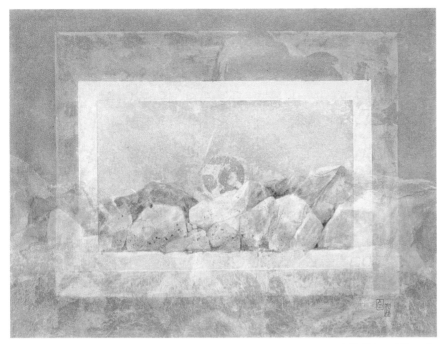

Although Marge Moore uses high-keyed colors and only a few dark accents, her rocks are convincing in their form and illusion of volume. In this painting, by letting the rocks break through a border shape, she creates a surreal effect, which is strengthened by the dominant gold color and feeling of transparency. In places there is a shimmering effect, developed by decollaging—tearing pieces of paper off the sheet after they were glued on and painted.

EREHWON III, by Marge Moore. Watercolor and collage, 22" × 30" (56 × 76 cm). Private collection.

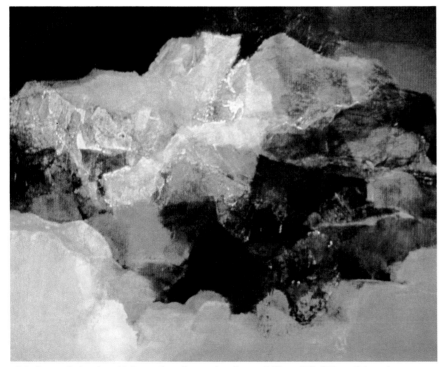

To build this complex surface, Lyn Keirns collaged torn pieces of acrylic-stained Oriental papers over each other. The layered and overlapping papers suggested rock forms and other natural features, which she emphasized with her brushwork. By leaving exposed fibers and letting colors show through some papers, she took full advantage of the physical properties of the various kinds of paper. Her visual statement reflects a sheer love of the collage medium and a willingness to explore the unpredictable aspects of collage techniques.

ICE ISLAND, by Lyn Keirns. Acrylic and collage, 20" × 25" (51 × 64 cm). Private collection.

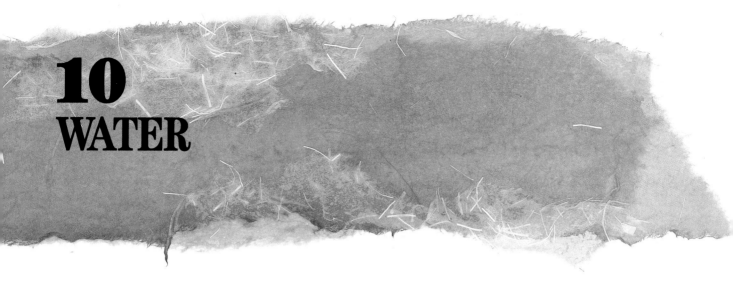

10 WATER

When you think of water in paintings, you may conjure up an image of crashing surf; a tumbling cascade; a quiet, reflective pool; or an idyllic cove. When Oriental papers are used in preparing the painting ground, however, it is most appropriate if the water is sloshing, splashing, tumbling, cascading, or otherwise in motion. Although it is possible to portray water that is smooth, still, and calm with collage, the painting process is more difficult. Most of the illustrations included in this chapter thus deal with rushing water in some form, and they show how collage techniques can greatly enhance both the working process and the final product.

Depicting rushing water necessitates generalization, abstraction, and simplification. The faster water moves, the less defined it appears to our eyes. The out-of-focus blur that is often associated with photographs of tumbling water finds its counterpart in unfocused white or off-white shapes in a painting. Such textured slashes can be dramatically enhanced with collaged Oriental papers to produce water images that are incredibly active in their visual impact.

Turbulent water can be handled in several ways—from extreme realism to an impressionistic image to pure abstraction. When working with collage techniques, however, you should try to stay loose for a time and let the developments on the surface help determine your approach to the subject. You might, for example, begin working on a shoreline subject with the intention of presenting a realistic image, but find that after the Oriental papers have been collaged, a stylized or abstracted feeling is projected. You must then make a decision about which course to pursue, although you should remain open to changes in direction as the work proceeds.

This is a traditional approach to painting a coastal subject, but the textured papers give it a quality unlike traditional watercolor painting. Collaged papers are evident in the surging storm surf and in the water tumbling over the foreground rocks. The fibers in some of the white papers create the visual impression of rivulets of water finding their way between and across storm-battered rocks. In addition, color showing through collaged papers produces the feeling of rocks showing through tumbling water.

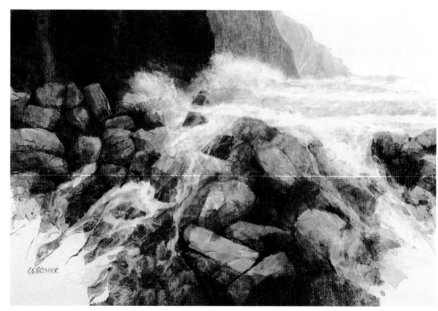

NA PALI COAST. Watercolor and collage, 15" × 22" (38 × 56 cm). Private collection.

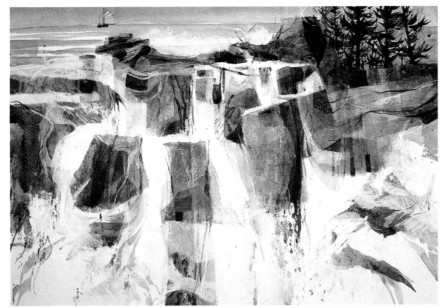

For this view of Japan's Inland Sea, I chose a high horizon to focus attention on the foreground rocks and water. As I added the collaged papers, the squarish, stylized shapes asserted themselves, and this abstract quality became a dominant feature. Notice that the collaged papers are not painted out or disguised; instead, their textures and fibers are left to be enjoyed by viewers. The dark, linear calligraphy supports and enhances the physical characteristics of the papers.

INLAND SEA. Watercolor and collage, 15″ × 22″ (38 × 56 cm). Collection of Mr. and Mrs. Jerome DiMaggio.

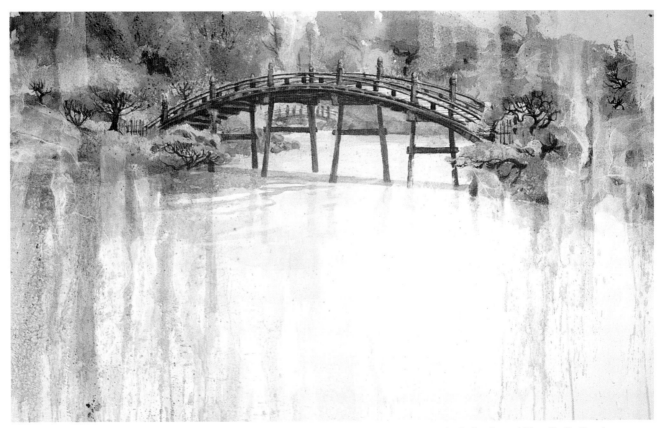

RITSURIN GARDENS/TAKAMATSU. Watercolor and collage, 22″ × 30″ (56 × 76 cm). Collection of Mrs. O. G. Pardue.

Although, generally speaking, it is best not to use collage when working with calm, reflective water, sometimes collage can enhance a particular mood. In this example of a Japanese garden in a gentle rain, the vertically adhered papers suggest the falling rain, while the variety of greens emphasizes the cool, rainy atmosphere. After first painting the water completely, I collaged a variety of thin papers over it, uniting the surface of the smooth water with the trees in the middle ground. I added a small amount of color to the collaged surface in a few places, but left most areas unpainted. When describing water, color showing through the collaged paper can often be more effective than color brushed over the textured surface.

PORTRAYING THE COASTAL SURF

One of the most exciting places to observe moving water is along a rocky coast. There the powerful confrontation between the crashing surf and the solid rocks provides excellent subject matter for paintings in which collage techniques are used. By overlapping various fibered white papers, you can capture the tumbling, writhing, sloshing movement of water in an amazingly vivid way. Let your initial color applications show through the collaged papers to provide the sensation of depth; then use paint on top of the papers to add local color and suggest shadows.

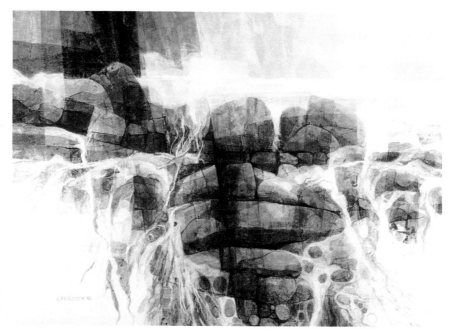

NA PALI IMPRESSION. Watercolor and collage, 22" × 30" (56 × 76 cm). Collection of R. H. Kellen.

This painting is based on the painting shown on page 106; it is an example of using another painting as a visual resource. Initially, I intended to make this work quite similar to the source painting, but as I drew the scene on the paper, slightly slanted lines began to dominate. This linear concept then guided my application of the initial paint and papers, as well as the design of the rocks, spray, cliffs, and water.

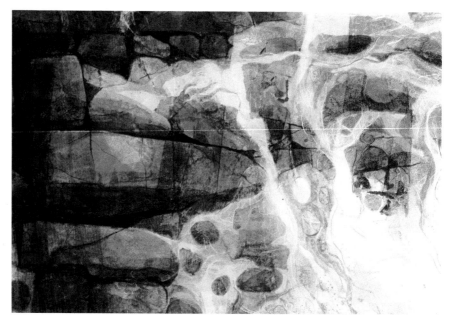

In the detail you can see how the buildup of fibers from several layers gives the feeling of water pouring over the rocks. Note the gradual transition in the design quality of rocks and water, from abstraction to realism.

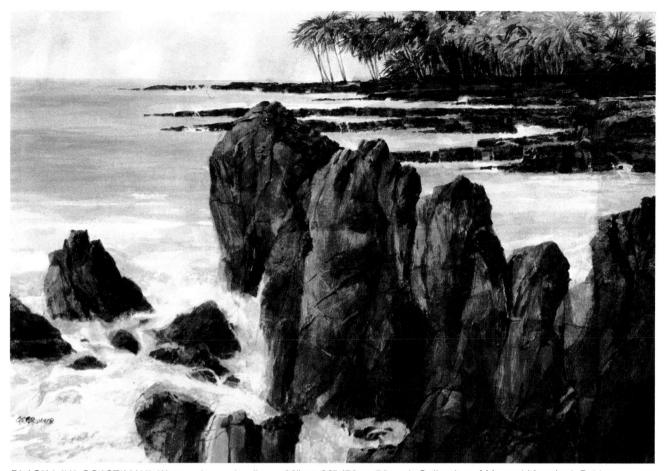

BLACK LAVA COAST/MAUI. Watercolor and collage, 22" × 30" (56 × 76 cm). Collection of Mr. and Mrs. Jack Fuhler.

Although the distinctive lava rocks of the Maui coast domi-nate this painting, the active white water acts as a perfect foil for the solid, unmoving rocks. When I began this painting, I did not intend to use collage, but as the work developed, the rocks did not acquire a sufficiently distinctive character. To establish a textural dominance, I thus added collage, from the base of the palm trees to the large rocks and foreground water. Then, with the overpainting, I emphasized the texture and brought out the local color in both the rock and water areas.

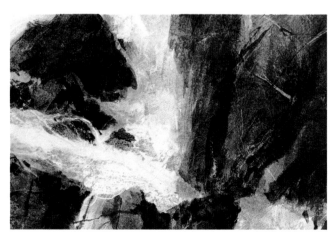

This detail illustrates the impression of depth created by painting under and over collaged papers. The painterly treatment suggests both the softness of water and the hardness of rock.

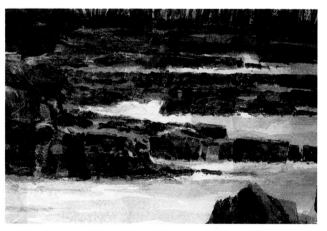

In this closeup of the right middle ground, the water and rocks are treated differently, because details would not be evident at such a distance. Even here, however, the papers suggest churning movement and the fluid action of the water, in contrast to the solid rock ledges.

CAPTURING CASCADING WATER AND ROCKS

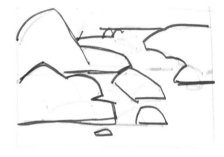

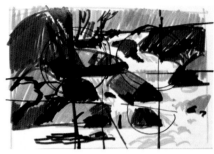

The subject for this demonstration is a segment of a tumbling river in Yosemite National Park. First, I simplified the complex arrangement of solid boulders and plunging white water into a few large, basic shapes in a sketchbook drawing. Then, using several marker pens, in three values of gray, I blocked in the major value shapes and divided my drawing into a tic-tac-toe format to tentatively locate a center of interest. With this design concept as a guide, I drew the large rock shapes in pencil on a full watercolor sheet and quickly painted the gray rocks and indicated some color in the water. When this was dry, I collaged the entire surface with a variety of Oriental papers.

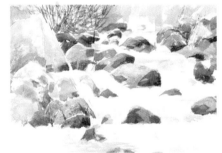

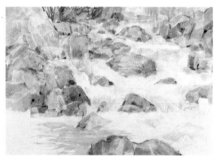

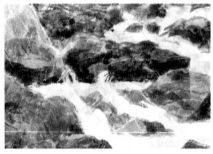

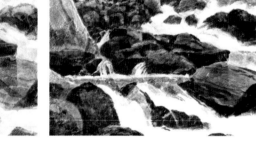

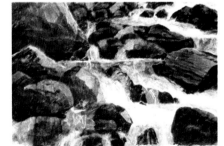

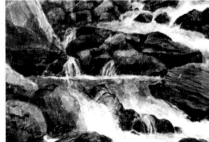

These four details provide a closeup look at how one part of the painting was built up. On the far left, in my first application of watercolor over the collage, I used light values of local colors to define rock shapes and begin to develop form, but did not tone the white water. In the next step, I further defined the forms, darkened values to approach those in nature, added a bit of warm color to the rocks, and toned the water in a few places. Then I collaged additional papers over parts of both the rocks and water to establish passage between the two major elements and to build complex textural areas. Finally, I again painted the surface, using various treatments for the water (direct color, scumbling, line—all drybrushed).

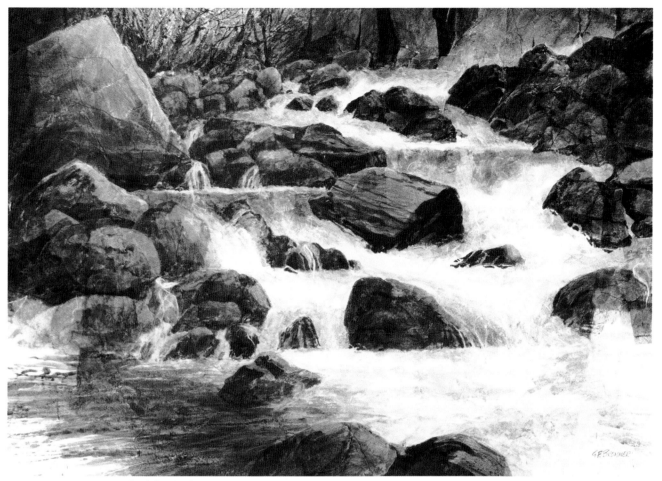

BELOW VERNAL FALLS/YOSEMITE. Watercolor and collage, 22" × 30" (56 × 76 cm). Collection of Mr. and Mrs. D. Holmes.

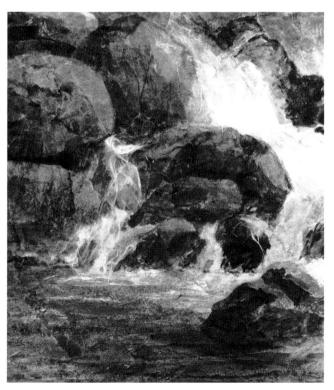

The finished painting reflects both the chaotic complexity of the original location and the attempt at organization begun in the sketches above. The rushing, tumbling, and swirling water is not painted very much. Instead, the rocks are made to look extremely hard, solid, textured, and heavy. The water, by contrast, seems light, liquid, and in motion. Remember that too much detail in water slows down visual movement, whereas a blurry, undetailed look implies rapid movement.

Notice how color is used in the water: whites imply foam and turbulence, as well as the light dancing off these surfaces; gray-greens signify slower movement and less turbulence; warm grays indicate rocks under tumbling water; and cool grays suggest shadows.

In this detail you can see the effect of the collaged papers on both the rocks and the water. The papers that simulate the tumbling water on the left were added over the finished rocks. Although several layers of paper were used for both the rock and water areas, the papers were always painted around the edges or toned in some way to visually work them back into the fabric of the surface. Note the effect of powerful value contrasts in establishing the hardness of the rocks and the fluidity of the water.

PERSONAL APPROACHES TO WATER

Water is found in many forms in nature and in diverse kinds of movement. When you combine this variety with the myriad techniques and styles of different artists, the personal approaches to the subject defy counting. The works shown on these pages do not illustrate all the ways to depict water, but they do provide a small sampling of the varied possibilities. As you continue to hone your painting skills, explore many different directions to find your own way of making a convincing visual statement.

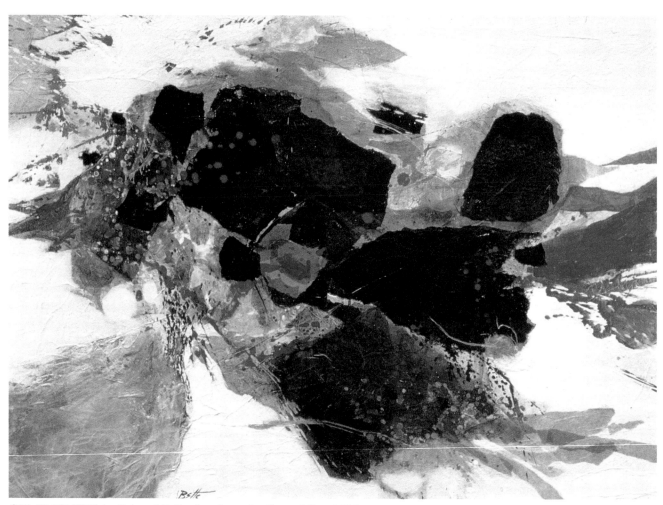

SEA FRAGMENT, by Edward Betts. Acrylic and collage, 21" × 30" (53 × 76 cm). Private collection.

In Edward Betts's words, he used collage in this work to establish "a complex interplay of transparent and opaque passages, or alternations of paper and paint, until the whole surface was fully orchestrated as an experience in shape, color, and texture." The subject matter of sea and rocks was incidental to this concept. He selected black Oriental papers and a variety of other Oriental papers, from very thin to heavily fibered. Some of these he stained with acrylic paints before collaging them, but others he left white. In some areas he brushed acrylics over this surface, but he also splashed and flung paint to create textural contrasts and color accents.

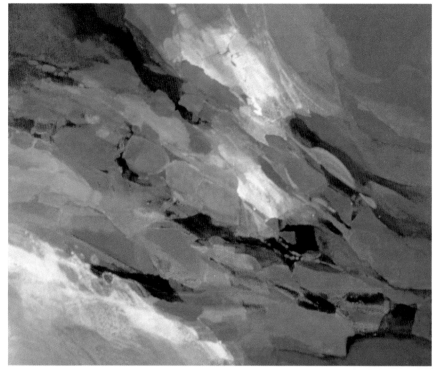

SEA CLIFF WATERS, by Lyn Keirns. Acrylic and collage, 17" × 22" (43 × 56 cm). Private collection.

Lyn Keirns developed this dramatic presentation of coastal waters with layers of collaged papers and acrylic paint. She stained many papers before collaging them to the surface, but she also painted over many of them, almost covering them up. In the finished work, some paper shapes and textures remain visible, while others are completely integrated into the surface. Notice the variety of sizes, shapes, and warm and cool colors. The water slashes against the coastal cliffs, establishing a surging rhythm and a striking color dominance.

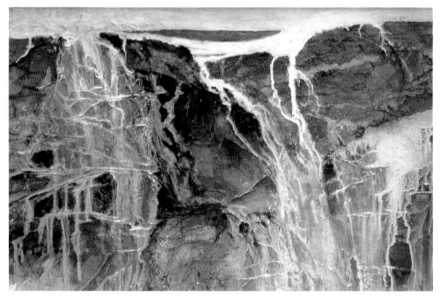

KY THAW, by Cecilia Slusser. Acrylic, ink, foil, and collage, 26" × 36" (66 × 91 cm). Private collection.

Cecilia Slusser enjoys letting the unexpected happen while building her surfaces, which she starts without any preconceived ideas. She began this painting by pouring paint on wet paper and allowing it to dry. Then she collaged several kinds of crushed Oriental paper with matte medium and continued to layer gesso, acrylic colors, and more papers (allowing each layer to dry) until she liked the complexity of the surface. Only then did she begin to tie the surface together and pick out a possible subject. Using more papers, acrylics, and ink, she defined the suggested subject and brought it to its culmination.

11 FOLIAGE

Leaves come in an incredible variety of textures, sizes, shapes, and colors, and landscape artists must learn to cope with all these variables in their work. Look carefully at different kinds of foliage and note the physical characteristics of each. Do the leaves seem soft or crisp? Are they sticklike or pliant? Can they best be painted with line or shape? What colors are they in sunshine, as opposed to an overcast sky or deep shadow? How do they differ from other leaves in their immediate environment?

Notice that, from a distance, leaves seem to mass together into large, simplified shapes, but, when seen closeup, they are often best described by calligraphic line. Also observe different kinds of leaves: from thin needles to flat, round shapes; from tiny to gigantic; from smooth-edged to serrated. It is a good idea to fill pages of your sketchbook with leaves drawn in a variety of ways. Since it is impossible to put on paper all the details in every tree, bush, or plant, you must learn to make marks that record characteristic generalities. This is true if you are working with collage techniques, direct watercolor, or any other medium. If you can develop a shorthand for describing different kinds of leaves (both singly and in masses), your skill in painting foliage will increase.

Because color is an important aspect of painting foliage, you must also learn to distinguish different greens. Of course, there are times of the year when the color of foliage changes, and there are trees that never have green leaves. But it is the color green that presents the greatest challenge. Leaf greens can be warm or cool, brownish or bluish, mixed with orange or yellow. Take a basic green color, such as Hooker's green light, and mix every other color in your palette with it to discover the variety of greens available to you. Then, after you have experimented with the green pigments, explore the range of blue and yellow mixtures. With all these possible greens, you are not restricted to tube colors, and you can avoid monotonous or uninteresting paintings of foliage.

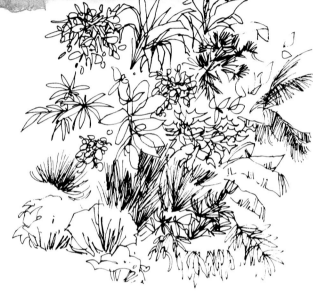

Fill sketchbook pages with leaves drawn from observation or from memory (such as these). Use line and value to explore different ways of drawing various kinds of leaves.

These pine trees show a variety of color, made by mixing greens with other hues. Light and shade also affect the colors in each tree. Note the typical limb structure of the pine trees and how the foliage is massed in large shapes, but also detailed, with individual needles and clusters, in places. In the background, the aspen leaves are a variety of yellows, massed together into large shapes.

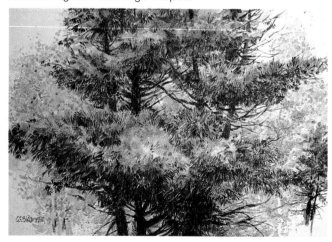

PINES AND ASPEN. Watercolor and collage, 15" × 22" (38 × 56 cm). Courtesy of Rosequist Galleries, Tucson, Arizona.

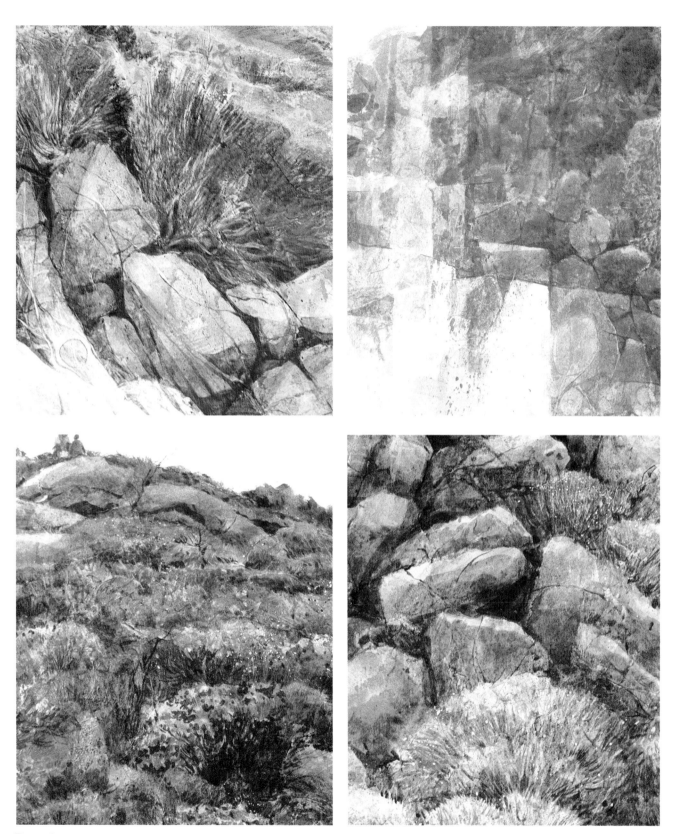

These four details, from four different watercolor and collage paintings, illustrate a variety of foliage textures. The calligraphic marks differ with the kinds of plants and their distance from the viewer. Notice, for example, how opaque white has been flicked on the surface to suggest white flowers. In other examples, the fibers of the papers play an important part in creating the feeling of texture.

SEEING FOLIAGE
AS COLORED TEXTURE

When foliage is seen at a distance, the textures are minimal. Nearly flat, greenish shapes can be used to depict trees on far-away hillsides. The focus should be on characteristic colors and unified shapes, rather than on details of single trees or bushes.

In a closeup view, however, you should look for characteristic textures to represent specific trees or other plant life. Although Oriental papers provide many interesting textures, they often need to be supplemented by brushwork. After careful observation and some drawing practice, you should be able to indicate grass, leaves, flowers, shrubs, trees, and other plants with special brushmarks. If you are doing a landscape painting, the plants do not have to be botanically exact, since the painting is far more important than the plants. You should, however, pay attention to the characteristic colors and textures of the plants, because they often provide the specific visual identity of a particular location.

When you are working with many kinds of foliage, remember to carefully observe both colors and textures before you make your plans for simplification, generalization, and calligraphic interpretation. You can use collaged papers to create a marvelous textural surface, but you must be able to incorporate these textures into your painting of foliage and add the kinds of marks that will describe the distinctive characteristics of each type of foliage.

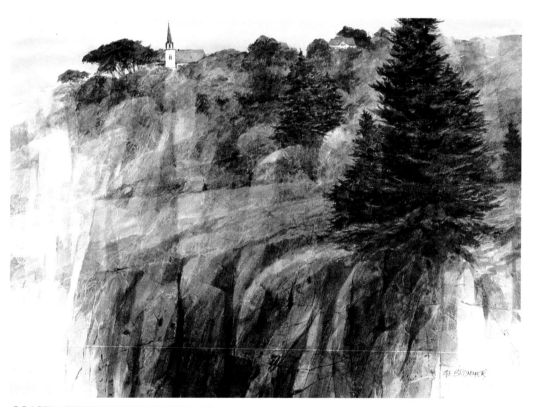

COASTAL TEXTURES/MENDOCINO. Watercolor and collage, 22" × 30" (56 × 76 cm). Collection of Dr. and Mrs. Frank Newman.

The dense foliage along the northern California coast is the dominant element in this painting. Note the variety of greens and the slight variation in textures on the middle-distant hillside. The nearest evergreen trees are more detailed than similar trees in the middle distance. The gradual decrease in detail from foreground to background provides a visual transition, creating movement into the picture. There is also a contrast between the soft edges of the tree shapes and the crisp edges of the foreground cliffs. The shafts of light on both sides of the painting help establish the sensation of pale sunshine showing through the coastal fog typical of this location.

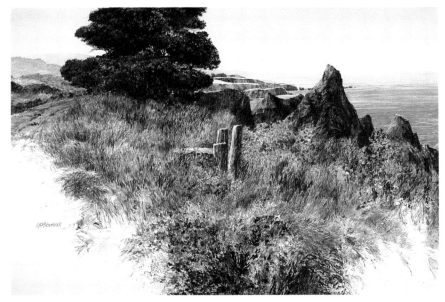

*THE PACIFIC COAST AT BIG SUR.
Watercolor, gouache, and collage,
30" × 40" (76 × 102 cm). Collection of
Technology Venture Investors, Menlo
Park, California.*

*The marvelously rich textural variety of
the foreground triggered my visual
response to this location. I wanted the
delicate quality and subtle colors of the
foliage to hold their own against the
grandeur of the Big Sur coastline.
Initially I used brushes and sponges
over the collaged ground and then
developed individual textural characteristics with calligraphic brushstrokes. To
suggest flowers and highlights, I spattered and brushed opaque white
gouache in places. By controlling the
light values, I established movement
patterns through the otherwise chaotic
foliage.*

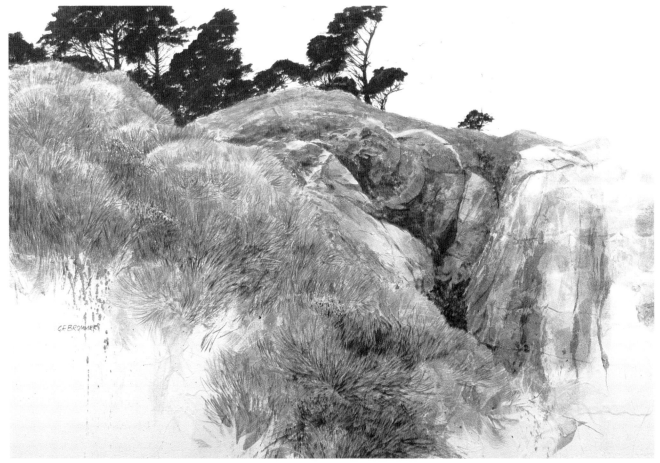

POINT LOBOS HILLSIDE. Watercolor and collage, 22" × 30" (56 × 78 cm). Collection of Mr. and Mrs. Rex Warden.

*Thin, grasslike lines, painted over collaged Oriental papers,
lend a textural quality to this hillside. The gradual transition
from closeup, implied detail to almost flat shapes at the crest
of the hill suggests space and distance. The soft foliage is
punctuated in places by flowering plants, which help to
direct eye movement over the hillside. The crisp-edged*
*rocks further emphasize the soft foliage of the grassy hillside
and provide textural relief and variety. At the top, the dark
tree shapes not only stop the vertical visual movement, but
also help to define the location of this central California
coastal scene.*

DEPICTING A REDWOOD FOREST

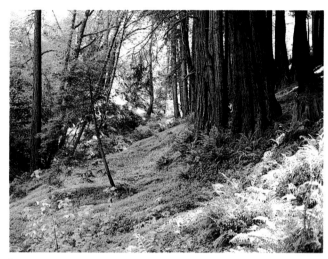

This photograph of a small redwood grove, north of Big Sur in central California, provides the basic resource material for the painting in this demonstration.

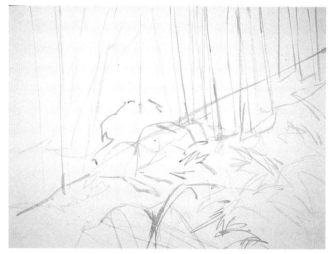

Using a large, pointed brush, I first loosely sketch the subject on the paper. Notice that I add some rock shapes to create visual variety and interest on the fern-covered hillside.

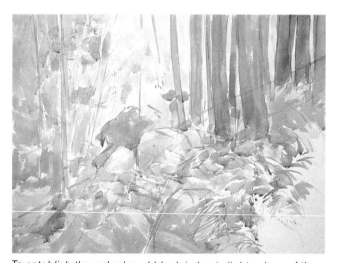

To establish the color key, I block in basic light values of the local colors.

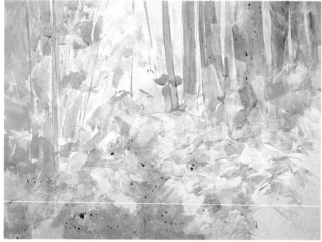

Next I collage the hillside and redwood trunks with Oriental papers, but not the delicate background light. Color shows through the papers, but the textures suggest a direction for the painting that differs from the original photograph.

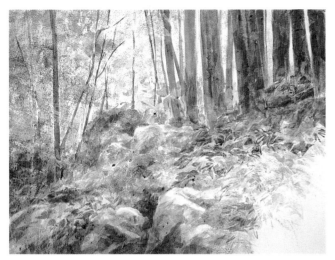

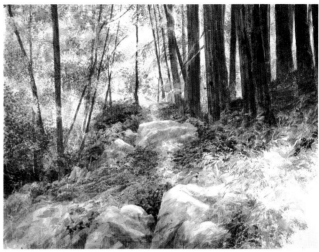

Using sponges, I print textures both in the background and on the forest floor. I also drybrush color on the collaged surface to establish the major visual elements: rocks, foliage, and tree trunks. After several layers of color have been applied, the pattern of light and shadow begins to exert itself.

To make the background light a foil for the shadowed foreground, I strengthen it with additional textural sponge printing. I also clarify the passage of light from negative space into the central core of the picture and glaze over shadows to make them deeper and richer.

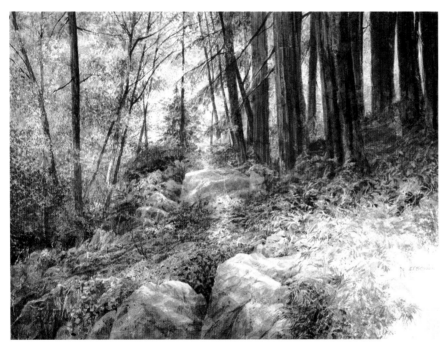

By pulling glazes over the background, I gray the outer edges and concentrate the glowing light above the light pattern in the foreground, tying these parts of the surface together. In other areas I use glazes of various colors and values to weave the painting together through the movement of light and dark. Final touches give the tree trunks a redwood-like quality and relate the background trees to the strong shadows. The result is a richly textured, foliage-covered hillside, with the quality of light typical of redwood forests. Compare this with the original photograph to see how the control of the light pattern and the added color and rocks create visual interest and direction in the painting.

BIG SUR REDWOODS. Watercolor and collage, 30" × 40" (76 × 102 cm). Courtesy of Fireside Gallery, Carmel, California.

DESCRIBING FLOWERS

Flowers can be incidental or vitally important elements in a landscape painting; they can be featured in a floral painting or serve as part of a still life setup. In general, because the textural qualities of flowers are similar to those of foliage, you can use collage techniques in much the same way for both—except for the application of color.

If you want to make floral paintings with collage, consider staining the papers before collaging them to the surface. You can also underpaint with watercolor (as in typical landscape techniques) and collage Oriental papers over the surface. Experiment with combinations of these and other collage processes to discover the most appropriate techniques for particular flowers.

When you are incorporating flowers in a landscape subject, take care to treat the flowers so they appear comfortable in their environment. The colors, for instance, should not jump forward to grab the viewer's attention, unless that is your intent. You may be surprised, however, to find that you need to exaggerate the colors in both area and intensity to convey their effect. If, for example, a few bright flowers stand out dramatically in a green foliage environment, you may have to spread the colors out in the painting to capture an impression similar to what you see in nature.

As with foliage, flowers can be massed together or seen individually. If you begin by painting on location, squint your eyes to become aware of the actual proportion of visual interest the flowers demand. Often, flowers can be grouped together and painted as colored shapes or forms, without a lot of detail.

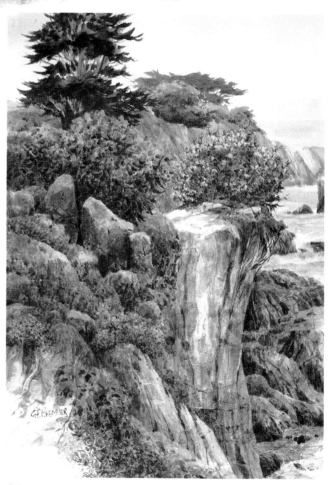

COASTAL TEXTURES/MONTEREY. Watercolor and collage, 30" × 22" (76 × 56 cm). Collection of Martha Selig.

The vivid colors of the flowered coastline of Monterey Bay are featured in this painting. Collaged Oriental papers provide a textural base for the water, rocks, foliage, and flowers. The flowers themselves are handled as massed color, punctuated with highlights and shadows to transform them from flat shapes into rounded forms. Although some blossoms are painted individually, they are always parts of plants and the entire scene, not individual entities.

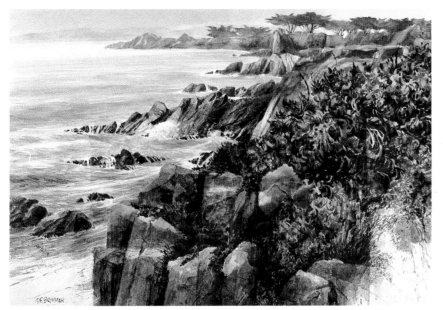

In this painting of Monterey Bay, the flowers are an important but incidental element. The feeling of pictorial depth is enhanced by the treatment of the flowers: the near foliage and flowers are painted as individual but generalized color elements, while the more distant pink flowers are seen as massed color shapes, diminishing in intensity as they get farther from the viewer. Also note the simplified, flat treatment of the distant rocks, trees, and water as a way to indicate depth and space. Very subtly, some of the flower colors are brushed into the rocks and water to relate these parts of the painting and to somewhat minimize warm and cool contrasts.

SPRINGTIME COAST/MONTEREY BAY. Watercolor and collage, 22″ × 30″ (56 × 76 cm). Courtesy of Fireside Gallery, Carmel, California.

The colorful flowers are vital to establishing a sense of place in this impression of the Kona Coast in Hawaii. Yet the flowers are not detailed; they are simply clumps of color. It is the feeling of mounds of vividly colored flowers that counts, rather than the individual representation of specific plants and flowers. Notice how the shadows on the flower forms produce a feeling of dimension and also create passage from the flowers to surrounding dark-value landscape elements.

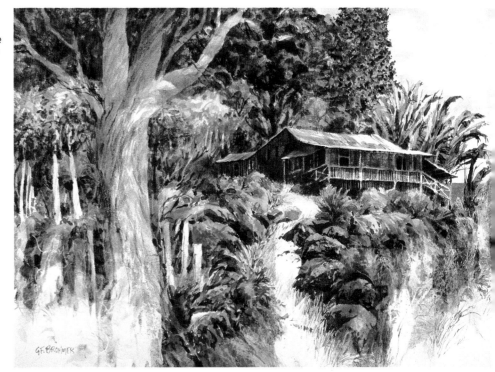

COASTAL PATTERNS/HAWAII. Watercolor and collage, 22″ × 30″ (56 × 76 cm). Courtesy of Esther Wells Collection, Laguna Beach, California.

12 SNOW AND FOG

Oriental papers can be used to help develop impressions of both snow and fog in your paintings. With a little experimentation and practice, you can collage opaque and medium-weight white papers over painted surfaces to create a cold or misty atmosphere. These collaged papers can be painted or left alone, allowing underpainted colors to show through, depending on the effect you want.

Because some Oriental papers are whiter than watercolor paper, their brilliance can be particularly effective in creating a snowy scene. You can work with opaque papers or build several layers of semi-opaque papers to get the quality of white you desire. You can also add opaque white paint to create the feeling of snow. Try designers gouache, casein, or gesso, either full-strength or diluted to some degree. You can even apply diluted whites so that they appear similar to thin veils of white Oriental paper.

Before experimenting with collaged papers to create a feeling of snow, however, look at paintings of snow in either oil or watercolor. Learn about the qualities of snow: its colors

in certain situations; its softness; its structure; how it reacts to sun, shadows, wind, and so on.

When depicting snow, take care to integrate it into the painting so it does not appear to be added on after the work was done. Make some value sketches to determine how to place the darks and lights in an interesting compositional arrangement. It is also a good idea, when you are tearing the white paper for a collaged snowscape, to make the pieces larger than you will need. By painting over the edges of these larger shapes, you can visually integrate them into the surface of the collaged sheet.

Even if you use opaque papers, it is best to first paint some color (such as cobalt blue) in the snow areas and then collage the white papers over it. Whatever color shows through the papers will add depth and substance to the white. If you decide to paint over the white papers, start with subtle, high-keyed colors to avoid destroying the illusion of soft snow. Remember, you can always add more white paper or opaque white paint if necessary.

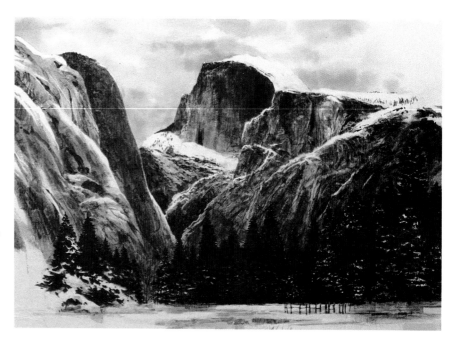

WINTER IMPRESSION/YOSEMITE. Watercolor and collage, 22" × 30" (56 × 76 cm). Collection of Carolyn Kille.

With collage, you can change a scene as you work. This impression of Half Dome in Yosemite National Park started as an autumn scene, but became a winter landscape as the painting developed. At first I painted all the cliffs, including the snow-covered areas, as though there would be no snow in the scene. As I collaged white papers onto this surface, however, a feeling of snow was introduced. Intrigued by this, I added opaque white papers to the tops of all the cliffs and ridges, as well as the trees and valley floor. When these papers were dry, I painted them at the edges to work them back into the surface. Notice that almost all the trees are painted, with only small white shapes of snow in the branches.

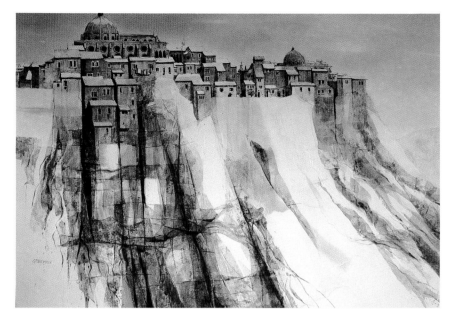

WINTER IN TUSCANY. Watercolor, ink, and collage, 22" × 30" (56 × 76 cm). Private collection.

To create this impression of a snow-draped village in central Italy, I first sketched the scene with pen and india ink. After laying in the initial watercolor washes, I collaged white Oriental papers and large, torn pieces of 300 lb. watercolor paper. I then left some white areas unpainted to indicate snow and worked these shapes into the cliff and village pattern. To emphasize the cold atmosphere, I grayed my colors; I also pulled warm glazes over selected areas to establish contrast. Using line, I then defined the building features and the crevices in the cliffs, and also created a transition between negative and positive elements in the lower corners.

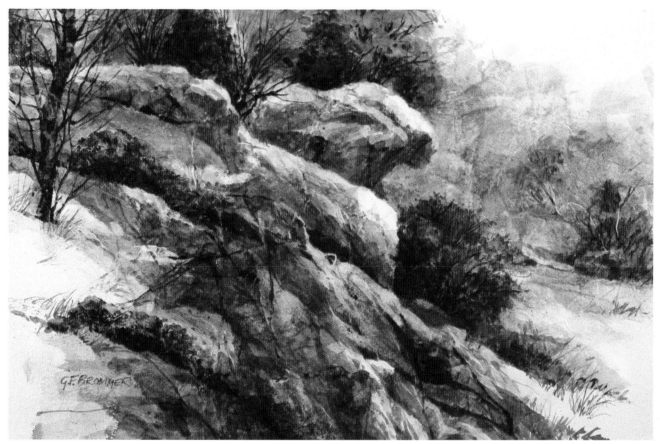

AUTUMN SNOWFALL/SIERRAS. Watercolor and collage, 15" × 22" (38 × 56 cm). Collection of Pacific Telesis Group, San Francisco, California.

This autumn landscape is an imaginary subject, developed from a small abstract collage, similar to those in Chapter 1. When the emerging colors suggested an autumn scene with touches of white snow, more opaque and semi-opaque white Oriental papers were added to enhance this impression. Notice that, in some areas, I pulled cool washes of grayed blue over snow shapes to suggest the forms underneath and to integrate the whites with surrounding areas. Remember that if papers seem to sit on top of the surface, you can add some paint to settle them into the surface. In general, the collage materials should not draw attention to themselves but should be part of the surface—fully integrated into the painting.

ACCENTING WHITE SNOW

How much snow you include in a landscape painting is entirely up to you and your interpretation of the scene. If you use transparent watercolor alone, of course, you must save white areas to indicate snow. With collage techniques, however, you can add whites to the painted surface, thus increasing the amount of snow at any time in the painting process. Then, if you want to decrease the amount of snow, you can simply paint over the white papers.

Experiment with different techniques. Try collaging torn pieces of 140 lb. or 300 lb. watercolor paper, or two- or three-ply Bristol paper, to provide basic white snow shapes. You can leave these as they are, or collage over them with Oriental papers.

When painting shadows or light-value colors in the snow areas, keep in mind that some of the opaque white Oriental papers are very absorbent, so you should use a very dry brush. If the surface is too absorbent and the colors splotch when they are added, try brushing an extra layer of diluted acrylic matte medium over the collaged papers to seal them. Experiment on some samples before trying this.

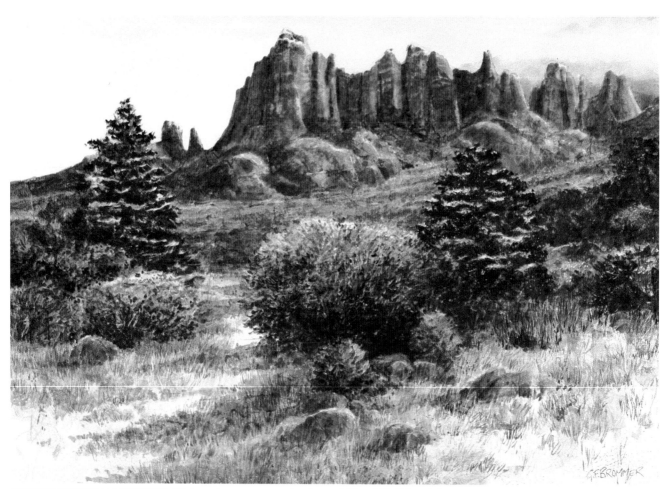

SPRING SNOWFALL/SEDONA. Watercolor, gesso, and collage, 22" × 30" (56 × 76 cm).
Courtesy of Aguajito del Sol Gallery, Sedona, Arizona.

A sudden spring snowfall in the Sedona area produced some chilly but magnificent contrasts. Working from a slide, I emphasized the cool, crisp morning light from the start. During the initial application of color, I left some white spaces to indicate snow and then collaged large areas with opaque white papers or several layers of semi-opaque papers. As I painted color back into these white spaces, I left the limited sparkle of a light snowfall. I also spattered and brushed diluted white gesso in places, to emphasize the feeling of newly fallen snow. Finally, I pulled shadows across the white areas to intensify the feeling of early morning light on the snow-dappled ground.

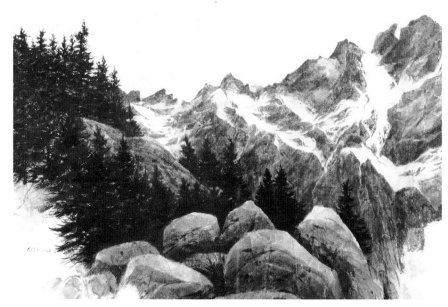

SIERRA RIDGE. Watercolor and collage, 15" × 22" (38 × 56 cm). Collection of Carolyn Boughton.

In this early spring scene, the snowy areas were collaged with opaque Oriental papers and then painted to leave patches of white. The dark accents of the evergreen trees provide a strong contrast so the whites glow with their own intensity. Observe the passage of light, which encourages visual movement from the sky into the mountains and from the negative space in the lower corners into the fully articulated areas of the painting. A sense of the distance between the viewer and the mountain is created by the change in scale from the trees to the mountain and by a lessening of color intensity in the mountain itself.

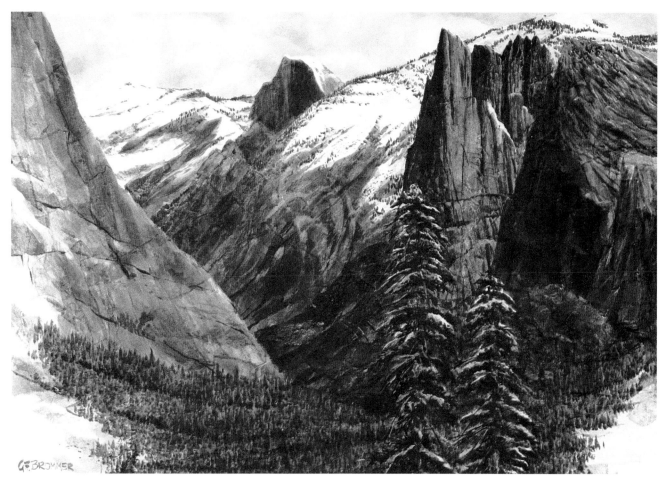

YOSEMITE VALLEY/EARLY SPRING. Watercolor and collage, 22" × 30" (56 × 76 cm). Collection of Mr. and Mrs. Roger McCollum.

Yosemite National Park is a breathtaking sight in early spring. Referring to slides and sketches, I composed the scene with two foreground trees to establish scale. When I collaged white papers over the painted surface, I used opaque varieties for the snowy areas. I then painted watercolor into the whites, but left the snow unpainted. Notice how the passage from the sky to the snow and the rocks simplifies this complex subject into several large shapes.

SUGGESTING A VEIL OF FOG

As you can see from the illustrations on these pages, Oriental papers collaged over lightly painted landscape elements can create a convincing sensation of fog. Experiment with a variety of papers to see which ones work best for foggy effects. Some of the thinner papers require three or more layers to push trees or a rocky coast into a misty distance. With other papers, one layer may be sufficient to create an atmosphere of fog.

If the foreground elements are fairly intense in color and value, the contrast with collaged and partially obliterated elements will suggest a veil of fog. When you paint over collaged areas, use a very dry brush and very light colors so that you only slightly intensify the colors. Of course if the colors in fog-shrouded areas become too intense, you can apply additional layers of paper to control the values.

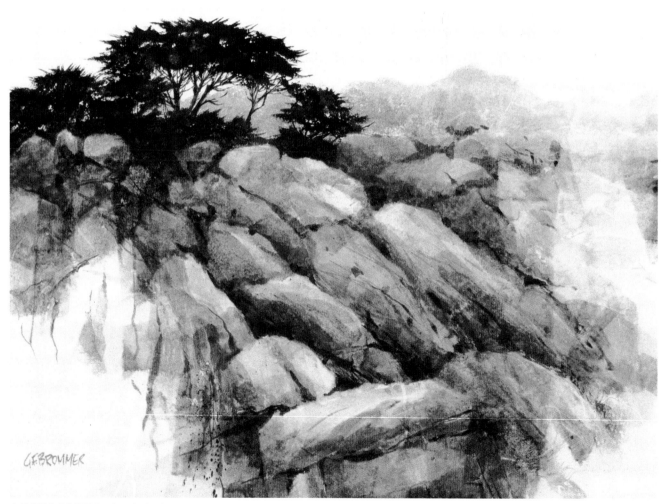

LOVERS POINT/PACIFIC GROVE. Watercolor and collage, 11" × 15" (28 × 38 cm). Collection of Mr. and Mrs. Douglas Purdy.

Although foggy forms are generally seen as flat shapes, they may have slight value variations. The distant trees in this small study were gently repainted with a dry brush and a neutral gray wash to suggest overlapping shapes at different distances from the viewer. Veils of light values then tie the foreground rocks to the distant trees, while the intense darks in the middle-ground trees help to define the distance between them. In most foggy landscapes, the sky can be left an unpainted white, or it can be given a light wash of gray.

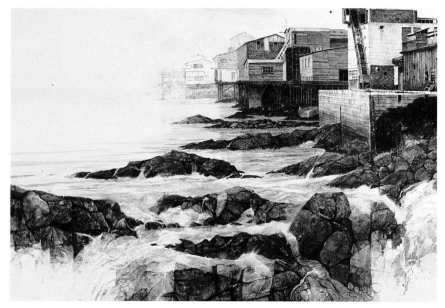

CANNERY ROW/MONTEREY. Watercolor and collage, 22" × 30" (56 × 76 cm). Collection of Bernard Brown.

The cool white of Oriental papers produces convincing fog effects, especially when combined with other methods of depicting depth and space. In this view of Cannery Row in Monterey, the distant buildings, shrouded in fog, were first painted and then covered with collaged Oriental papers of several kinds. The feeling of foggy light in the collaged area carries over into the direct watercolor treatment of the sky and the quiet waters of the bay. This cool light, however, gets warmer as it advances toward the viewer. Color and value intensity also increase in the foreground, where the rocks and water dramatically set the stage for the rest of the painting.

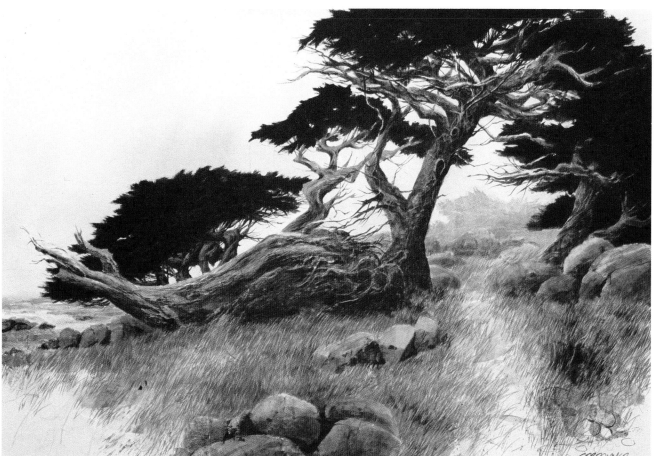

PATH TO THE SEA/CARMEL. Watercolor and collage, 22" × 30" (56 × 76 cm).   Collection of Mr. and Mrs. William Smith.

Here the background trees, shrouded in fog, are actually shrouded in collaged Oriental papers, which push them far into the distance. The abrupt change in value, from the foreground to the background trees, suggests a vast distance between the two. (In reality, it was about a quarter of a mile.) The flat, white sky enhances the sensation of fog, and the lack of definite shadows indicates an evenly diffused light, typical of a bright, foggy day. Note, however, that despite the sense of great distance from the foreground to the foggy background, there are still places of passage that lace the diverse elements of the painting together.

13 BUILDINGS

Because many Oriental papers have an organic surface quality, with curving fibers and torn edges, while most buildings are geometric in form, the two seem incompatible. But the organic qualities of the papers can prove extremely useful in depicting old buildings, crumbling ruins, or other weathered structures. If newer, more intact buildings are the subject, you might choose papers with few or no visible fibers and cut them with scissors or a knife to produce straight edges, suggestive of geometric structures.

Buildings can be treated as the dominant element in a painting or as part of a larger environment. You may wish to use collage on all, part, or none of the buildings. Whatever you decide, however, make sure the painting is unified. If you do not use collaged papers on the buildings, use similar textures, values, and colors to weave the painting together. And, if you do use collage, take care to fully integrate the structures into the painting so they do not appear cut out and pasted onto the surface.

Complete visual integration is easier to accomplish if you treat the entire surface (whether collaged or not) the same way, and if you paint the entire surface at the same time. Distribute colors, values, and textures used in the buildings throughout the painting whenever possible; also reflect aspects from surrounding elements in the buildings. Develop value passages from the buildings into the surrounding environment and pull similarly colored shadows over buildings and environmental elements. The idea is to make the painting work as a whole.

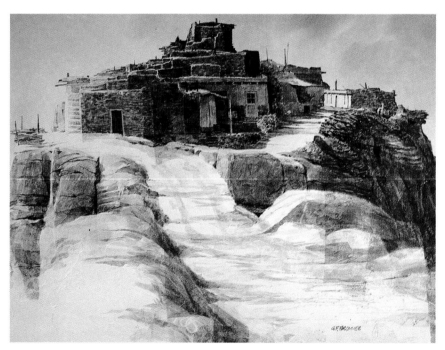

The textured, collaged buildings of this Hopi village and the supporting, wind-battered mesa are played against a smooth wet-in-wet sky. To establish the feeling of worn and crumbling edges, all the papers were torn rather than cut. The warm earth colors then enhance the feeling of a weathered, time-worn setting. At the same time the white and nearly white papers used for the light passage create a feeling of intense sunlight, which is augmented by the contrast of deep shadows.

WALPI VILLAGE/FIRST MESA. Watercolor and collage, 22" × 30" (56 × 76 cm). Collection of David Morris.

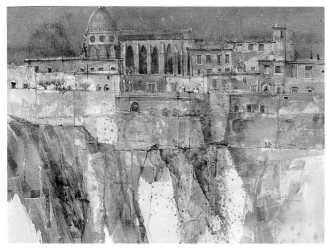

SPANISH HILLTOWN. Watercolor and collage, 22" × 28"
(56 × 71 cm). Collection of Home Savings of America,
Los Angeles, California.

Although the soft papers used in this work absorbed colors
in unpredictable ways, the surfaces of the buildings were
actually enriched by this. After the collage and painting had
dried, I used a pen and india and sepia inks to draw lines
and define shapes. In the detail, you can see the textures
created with paint and papers, as well as the line treatment.
Note the use of opaque white, which was drybrushed around
some windows to accent these sunlit surfaces.

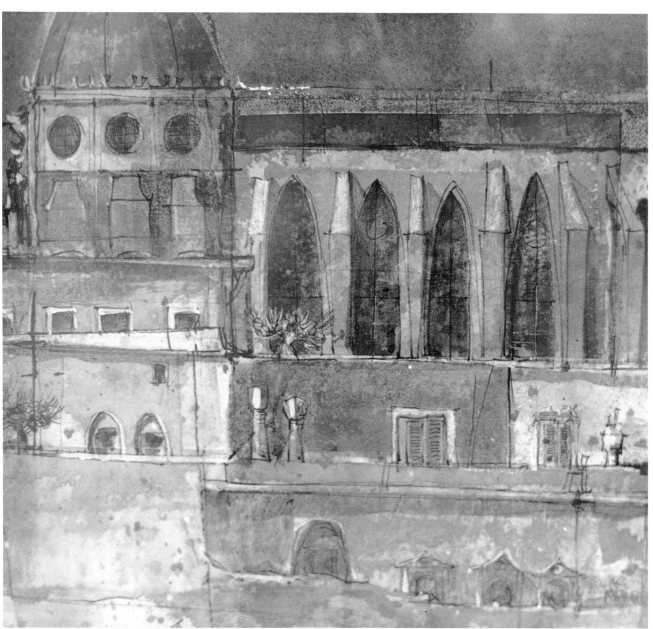

SITUATING BUILDINGS IN THE ENVIRONMENT

It is possible to make successful building paintings in which no environment is seen at all—where the entire surface is taken up with details of exterior walls. Most of the time, however, artists plan buildings in environmental settings to give them a sense of place. The amount of space taken up by the dominant structure varies, depending on the artist's decisions about composition.

Whatever the design, the painting as a whole should reflect your reaction to the building and its location in its environment. Think of the building as part of the environment and therefore part of the resulting painting. Work the two major elements (building and environment) together to make a single statement. Do not think of the building as a separate entity, removed from its environment—unless that is the impression you got from the original subject.

The three works on these pages illustrate different treatments of buildings in their environments. Each presents a total package, with unified elements. And, most important, each reflects the light, mood, texture, color, and overall visual impact of the original site.

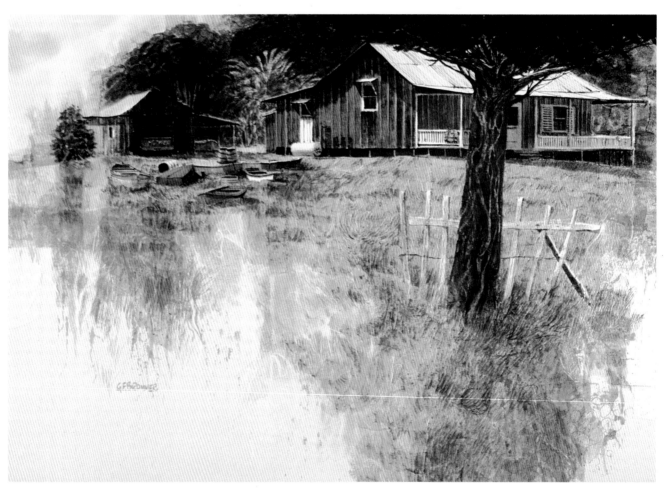

HANALEI IMPRESSION. Watercolor and collage, 22" × 30" (56 × 76 cm). Collection of Mr. and Mrs. William M. Herbert.

Although the Hawaiian cottage is a key ingredient in this painting, it takes up only a small fraction of the total space. Grass, earth, rain, and a jungle of Hawaiian trees share the surface with the buildings. The red cottage is as different in color as it could be, and yet it feels comfortable in its green surroundings. Notice how the building colors are scattered in varying intensities throughout the painting. There is also some green in the shadow colors of the building. Vertical shafts, both bold and subtle, help tie the parts of the painting together, as does the overall textural treatment. Despite many disparate parts, the painting has a prevailing sense of visual unity.

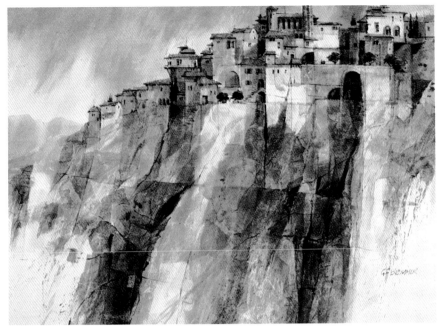

The overall quality and limited palette help unify the surface of this painting. The viewer's eyes move up the cliff faces to the village, where they are held by interlocking shapes and values, as well as the comparatively richer detail. Note how passages of color and value tie the structures solidly and irrevocably to the mountain, as if they were physically joined together. The buildings do not rest on the mountain, they are one with the mountain. The sky is purposely treated in a painterly way to make it visually compatible with the mountain. As you continue to look at the painting, you may be surprised to discover that the seemingly great amount of detail is more suggestive than actual; this feeling is enhanced by the lack of detail in much of the environment.

TUSCANY REMEMBERED. Watercolor and collage, 22″ × 30″ (56 × 76 cm). Courtesy of Fireside Gallery, Carmel, California.

The subject of Cannery Row is repeated several times in this book, but each painting presents a different emphasis. Here the buildings dominate, but they are still closely related to their coastal environment. Collaged papers were used in the water and rocks and part of the way up into the structures. The painting then ties the buildings irrevocably to their environment; indeed, it would be difficult to separate these two major pictorial elements.

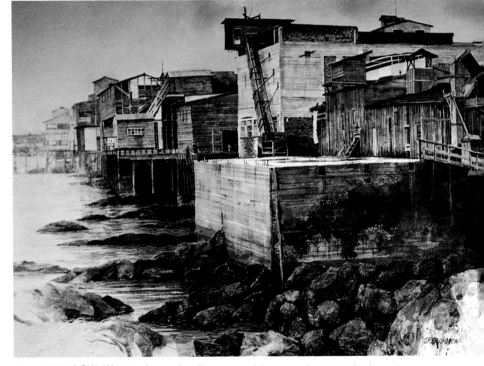

CANNERY ROW. Watercolor and collage on cold-pressed watercolor board, 24″ × 36″ (61 × 91 cm). Collection of David Morris.

DEVELOPING AN ONGOING THEME

Many artists are involved with ongoing themes, creating variations of a familiar subject. A series may be developed in successive paintings over a short period of time, or it can be a recurring theme, worked on at intervals over a span of many years. Reworking the same subject in this way can build confidence and encourage freedom. If you already know the subject intimately and have handled it in a variety of situations, you may be stimulated to explore new directions by changing the concept, style, treatment, emphasis, format, technique, mood, or color. With so many choices, the variety of approaches to a single subject can be almost endless.

The Italian hilltowns shown on these pages represent only a few of the many paintings I have done of this subject over a period of twenty years. Some have been direct watercolor, acrylic, or oil paintings, but most have combined the marvelously intricate textures of Oriental papers with watercolor. The series began with a group of direct paintings and drawings done on location in Tuscany and Umbria. After a year or so of working on the spot, as well as from sketches, slides, and photographs, I began to paint hilltowns that combined elements from a number of locations. The next step was logical—imaginary hilltowns began to grow on my paper. The final step was to simply put watercolor and collage on the paper and let the textures, values, and colors suggest the hilltowns and their settings. I then developed these impressions with a variety of concepts in mind.

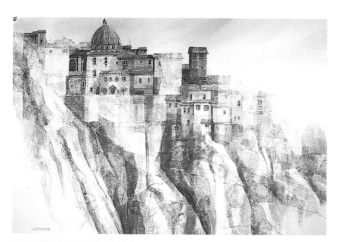

IMPRESSION OF TUSCANY. Watercolor, gesso, and collage, 22" × 30" (56 × 76 cm). Private collection.

All the buildings in this painting are imaginary, although some are based on observed building shapes. At one point I thought I had finished the painting, but then realized it lacked depth and surface variation. By collaging another layer of Oriental papers over parts of the painting, I was able to project a feeling of morning fog drifting through the town yet burning off under bright sunlight. I added a little color to the windows and structural surfaces, but retained the fog-shrouded feeling. I also added white gesso to the window frames and in several other places to visually tie the foggy whites to the buildings and hillside. The resulting painting is not what I originally planned, but it is compositionally much stronger than the initial "finished" stage was.

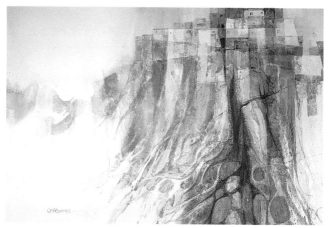

HILLTOWN PATTERN #4. Watercolor and collage, 15" × 22" (38 × 56 cm). Collection of James Powell.

Pattern and texture are featured in this hilltown impression. The initial rocklike textures were established by collaging Oriental papers and 300 lb. watercolor paper on the surface. Note that detail is practically eliminated as the rectangular, interlocking patterns of the perched village move down into the supporting cliffs. The brilliant, glaring sunlight provides a "reason" for this obliteration of detail and emphasis on the major patterns.

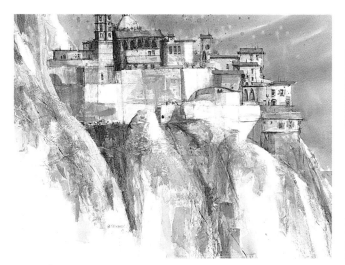

HILLTOWN IMPRESSION. Watercolor, gesso, ink, and collage on cold-pressed watercolor board, 22" × 30" (56 × 76 cm). Private collection.

To explore a different approach to my hilltown subject, I used a variety of media. After painting the scene on cold-pressed watercolor board, I used collaged papers and gesso to build up the surface in several layers, and then described details with pen and ink. By brushing watercolor over the gesso in places, I created a painterly surface, which adds to the textural impact of the work.

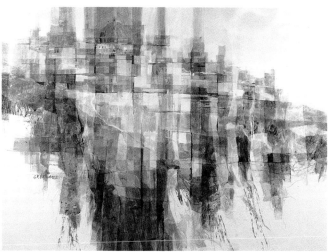

AUTUMN PATTERNS/TUSCANY. Watercolor and collage, 22" × 30" (56 × 76 cm). Collection of Dr. and Mrs. George Smith.

Here, after completing the initial painting and collaging, I directed the subsequent application of watercolor toward an emphasis on pattern. Although minimal detail suggests a hilltown subject, the mosaic-like patterning dominates. The color, limited to the earthtones that typify Italian hilltowns, helps establish a sense of place.

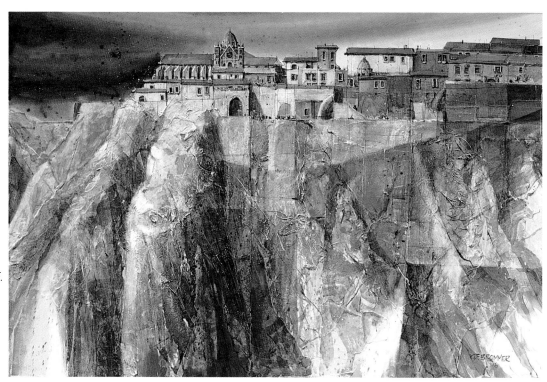

END OF THE CLIFF. Watercolor, gesso, ink, and collage on watercolor board, 24" × 36" (61 × 91 cm). Collection of the State of California.

Several actual buildings in different Italian towns were combined with imaginary structures to build this hilltown impression. But it is the large thrusting shape of the city and cliff that is the dominant element in the painting. The dramatic light emphasizes this dramatic setting. The collaged surface, which provides basic textural interest, is enriched by areas of drybrushed white gesso, which pick up and accent the textures. The heavy feeling of the buildings and cliffs, however, is lightened somewhat by the calligraphic ink line used to describe details and break up larger shapes.

FOCUSING ON
WEATHERED BUILDINGS

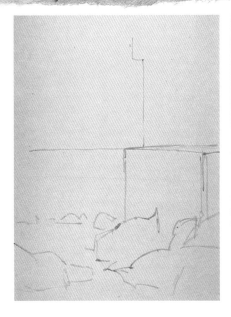

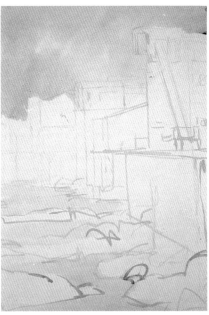

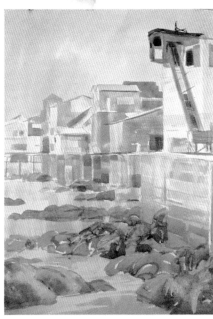

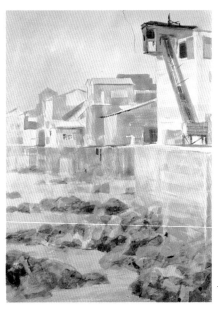

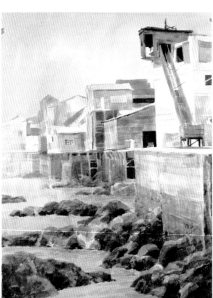

In addition to showing how to develop recognizable buildings, this demonstration provides a final review of the basic watercolor and collage process. I begin with a few basic vertical and horizontal lines to position the major elements and provide basic proportions. After completing my sketch, I sponge the sky area with water and lay in a pale gray-blue wash, working wet-in-wet. The sky color is repeated in the water. Next, I quickly brush in light values of local colors with a flat 1-inch brush. When this is dry, I collage pieces of torn Oriental paper over the lower half of the painting and up into some of the buildings. Then, I apply watercolor again, starting with light values and a fairly dry brush. Gradually, I build darker values in both the collaged and uncollaged areas, working over the entire surface at each stage.

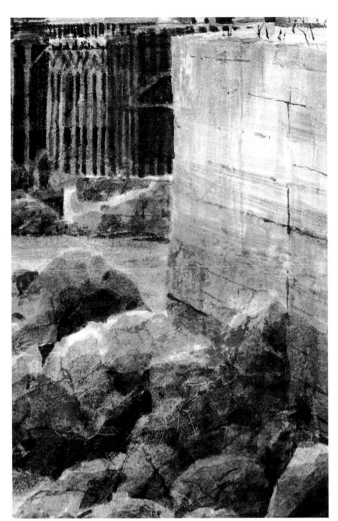

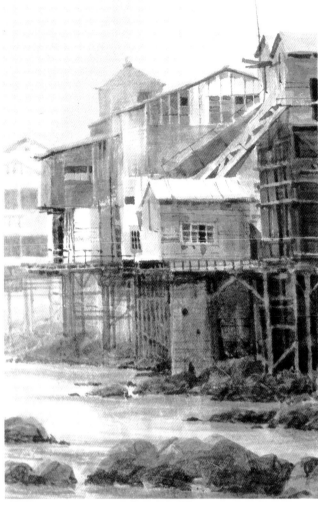

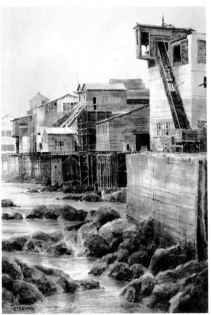

In the final painting and the details, you can see that implied textures in the directly painted areas have been keyed to the collaged areas to make these two parts visually compatible. Also notice that some building colors are reflected in the rocks to foster unity. To clarify the passage of light values, I lifted color in a few places, while I strengthened the dark and middle-value passages by glazing. Throughout, however, I took care to keep the colors subdued to suggest a "foggy-bright" atmosphere.

STRUCTURE PATTERN/CANNERY ROW. Watercolor and collage, 30" × 22" (76 × 56 cm). Collection of Dr. and Mrs. Wendell Brown.

14
GENERATING FREEDOM OF EXPRESSION

Manipulating new and varied materials tends to have a freeing influence on the spirit and working techniques of most artists. The collage process gives painters the opportunity to explore new directions without actually changing media. Although this book has focused on the combination of transparent watercolor and handmade Oriental papers, there are many other directions to be tried.

Each artist approaches collage with his or her own personal attitudes, concepts, and background, so individual approaches and products differ greatly. Several artists who work with collage and layering processes discuss their work and thoughts on the following pages. Perhaps looking at their work and reading about their ideas will encourage a new freedom of expression in your own work.

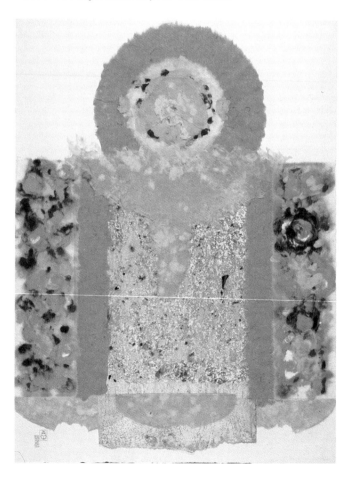

INCA WEAVE #2, by Marge Moore. Handmade papers and collage on 300 lb. cold-pressed paper, 30" × 22" (76 × 56 cm). Courtesy of the artist.

Marge Moore often uses Oriental papers and watercolor in her paintings, but she also explores other kinds of paper. In Inca Weave #2 she used two types of paper. As she describes it: "I make marbled papers from rolls of Sumi paper with oil and water, and also experiment with using water-soluble Marcus paints for the marbling technique. I keep a drawer full of these papers and add them to my Oriental papers wherever I can. These papers are made at random in all colors so that they have a spontaneity and uniqueness to add to the painting. The second textural addition is handmade paper, made from a variety of materials, and either stained or left a natural color."

Moore arranges and rearranges the torn papers until she is pleased with them, and then collages them to a sheet of 300 lb. cold-pressed watercolor paper. If necessary, she retouches some areas with watercolor, but the stained and marbled papers generally contain all the color and texture needed to complete the work.

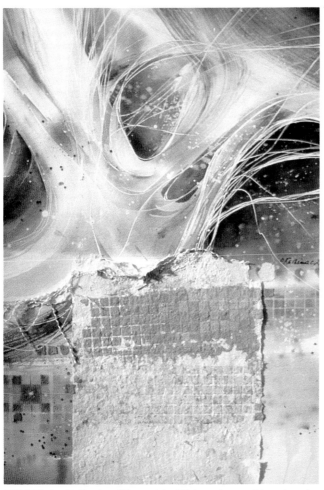

Katherine Liu uses a variety of papers in her collages—pieces of old paintings, monotypes, handmade papers, serigraphs, and Oriental papers. Weave started out as a direct watercolor dealing with mass and lines. Liu explains, "I was trying to have a spontaneous area balance a large geometric form at the bottom. The top of the painting was developed with layered washes, but the bottom lacked texture and did not connect well with the top. I wanted the bottom to imply a kind of woven fabric—a continuation of free-flowing fiber forms."

"The solution came," she says, "when I found a small piece of paper with hand-formed grids, which seemed just right for the 'woven fabric' effect. After several trials, I found a placement that would carry the two bands of washed watercolor through the handmade paper. Additional grid forms were painted on both sides of the paper to expand the design. By introducing a collaged paper, I was finally able to get the change of texture I wanted."

WEAVE, by Katherine Chang Liu. Watercolor and handmade paper collage, 30" × 22" (76 × 56 cm). Private collection.

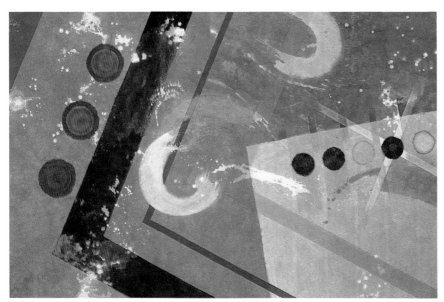

SIGNALS II, by Glenn R. Bradshaw. Casein, Oriental papers, and white glue, 37" × 57" (94 × 144 cm). Collection of the artist.

When Glenn Bradshaw uses several materials in combination, he tries to make one of them dominant. In this water-media collage, the painted portion is primary, while the collage elements (also painted) are subordinated and used to create variety. Different kinds of edges are achieved by wet-line tearing (making a wet line with a pointed brush and clear water, and then pulling the paper apart at this line) and by perforating the Oriental papers. The materials—diluted casein paint, paper, and glue—are kept simple to make sure the content of the painting remains more important than the technique.

Bradshaw notes, "Conceptually, my current work is nonobjective. It is concerned with the contrast between static and fluid forms, and may have symbols juxtaposed in an enigmatic way. But it has neither narrative nor message. It is intended to be an interesting visual adventure, to be enjoyed."

EXPLORING LANDSCAPE EXPRESSIONS

Freedom of expression can lead in many directions—from pure abstraction to realistic representation, and from emphasis on materials and techniques to emotional responses and conceptual approaches. Any book can only scratch the surface when exploring such a wide range of directions. The four artists represented on these two pages work with a variety of collage techniques to express their feelings about landscape elements. Collage encourages them to break from traditional approaches and deal with landscapes in unique ways.

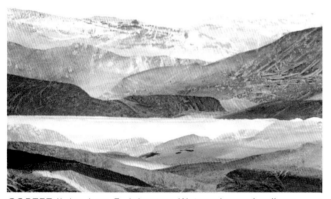

CORTEZ II, by June F. Johnston. Watercolor and collage, 28¹/₂" × 39¹/₂" (72 × 101 cm). Courtesy of the artist.

The arid mountains and beaches around the Sea of Cortez were the inspiration for this piece. There the cliffs and hills are varied in hue and intensity because of different mineral deposits and the ever-shifting light source. The textured earthforms provide a direct and powerful contrast to the soft sky and water.

For this painting, June Johnston painted sheets of watercolor paper and, when they were dry, tore them to create whatever shapes she desired. She then arranged the pieces on a backing sheet and permanently affixed them with hinges of linen tape. She explains, "I chose to emphasize the rich, natural colors by using very saturated paint in earthtones, reds, and blues, with several glazes laid on top of the original washes. The textured effects are achieved with plastic wrap, salt, and sprayed water."

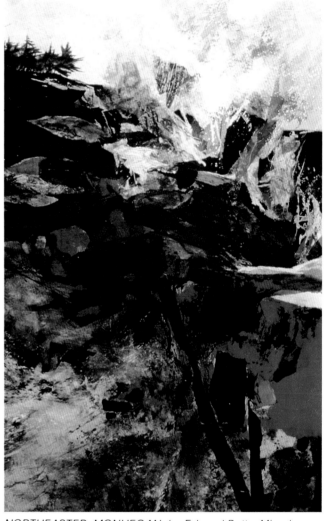

NORTHEASTER, MONHEGAN, by Edward Betts. Mixed water media and collage, 48" × 30" (122 × 76 cm). Private collection.

In the early stages of creating this powerful image, Edward Betts used collaged Oriental papers to build textures and suggest possible shapes and relationships. He alternated watercolor, collage, and acrylics until a possible direction suggested itself. He then used acrylics to paint over most of the surface, to the point that the collaged papers almost disappear. The collage is thus subservient to the whole.

"In this work," Betts explains, "I used collage in an improvisational approach, playing randomly with the interaction of collage and gestural paint application until the collage elements are no longer evident or identifiable as a method or as application. The viewer is not aware that collage has even been used until later scrutiny reveals it."

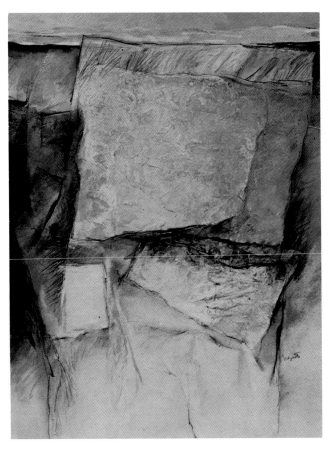

YELLOW DESERT CLIFFS, by Alexander Nepote. Water media and collage on Crescent watercolor board, 40" × 30" (102 × 76 cm). Private collection.

Alexander Nepote's cliff paintings are certainly a response to the natural environment, but they are much more than that. After sketching his ideas, he tears watercolor paper into large shapes, collages them on a heavy watercolor board, and applies washes of transparent watercolor. He continues layering paper and paint, and then sandpapers, cuts, and peels off segments to suggest flaking cliff surfaces and rock textures.

He comments, "I feel that the essence of art is the structure of relationships, which create within the painting the same interconnections found in nature. I sense that my responsibility as an artist is to create a new entity, based on my observation of nature and my intuitive feelings. In trying to express these insights, I discovered that working with layers of paper enabled me to achieve a unified whole. The actual physical technique of building a composition by adding layers made it possible to develop my concepts into meaningful paintings much more effectively than with the application of paint to a surface."

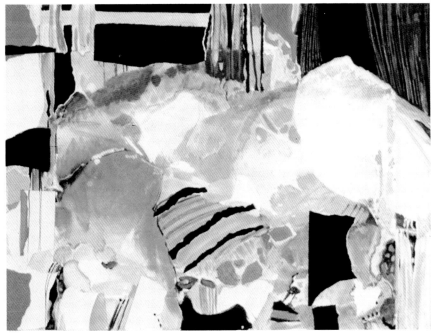

MOUNTAIN RIDGES, by Jeny Reynolds. Water media and collage, 30" × 40" (76 × 102 cm). Private collection.

This painting, constructed after a trip to Colorado, reflects Jeny Reynold's impression of snow-capped mountains. She states, "My attention was directed at the strong dark and light shapes hidden within the large masses. I tried to develop the rock shapes in a spontaneous manner, and picked up anything at hand that would express the lines, shapes, and color of the mountains as I remembered them. Oriental papers provided the textural quality, and paint was applied to some of the black and white shapes. Black shapes are both drawn and made from torn paper. Small cerulean blue accents hold the painting together and create color balance within the design."

"Emotion and enthusiasm are two important ingredients in my work," Reynolds asserts. "I am determined to allow what I see to merge with the feelings of my heart. Therefore I try to reveal an inward response, not a likeness of natural or physical forms."

DEVELOPING A CONCEPTUAL THEME

Some artists enjoy delving into new subjects with every painting they begin, while others like to work in a series, making many paintings around a single theme and discovering different solutions to the visual problems. The paintings on these two pages are single examples, removed from the continuity of a developing theme; but they grew out of the artists' exploration of a subject or idea in depth. When a series is developing well, each painting suggests a direction for the succeeding work.

If you have never worked in a series, take a favorite subject or concept and do five or ten paintings, either in succession or alternating them with other work. Working with a theme should encourage you to find different ways of looking at the same subject and expressing your responses.

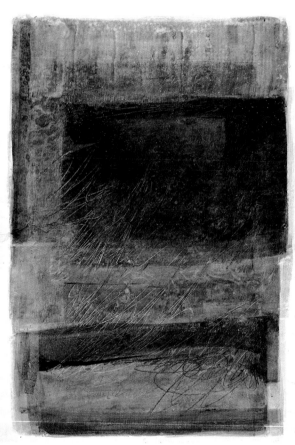

STONE SERIES 28, by Louise Cadillac. Watercolor, acrylic, and collage, 30" × 22" (76 × 56 cm). Private collection.

There are now more than fifty paintings in Louise Cadillac's Stone Series (for another work in this series, see page 78). Each is identifiable as part of the series, but each is also different in its individual expression. "In some pieces," Cadillac notes, "torn Oriental paper strips or bands may be used for their natural edges, and for the sensuous textures produced when paint bleeds and feathers as it seeps into the papers. Interesting and unexpected lines are formed as paint collects on the edges of the strips. Some lines are imperceptible except for the shadows they cast. Collage is used and enjoyed in these pieces as surface enrichment."

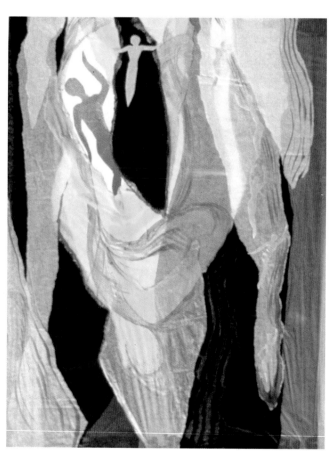

PASSAGES: CYCLE SERIES #5, by Mary Carroll Nelson. Acrylic, gold leaf, ink, and collage, 21" × 18" (61 × 46 cm). Collection of the artist.

Mary Carroll Nelson often works on several series at one time. This painting, she says, is part of a "series [that] continues off and on, dealing with the death motif and the changing of form. I made up a gold-leaf spirit form for the series that reappears all the time. It is gold leaf over something thicker, like handmade paper or matboard." At the same time Nelson is working on a series that deals with treasures. "The idea," she explains, "is that treasures are within, and hence are located within the piece."

140

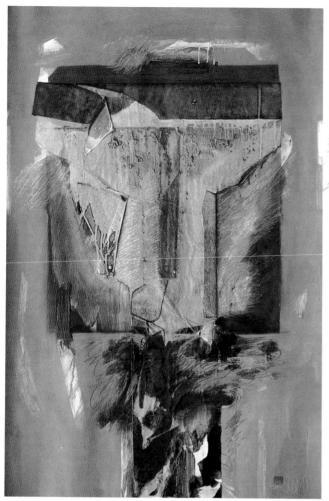

TC-77B, by Stanley G. Grosse. Mixed media and collage on paper, 40" × 26" (102 × 66 cm). Private collection.

Stanley Grosse gives his pieces numbers rather than titles to identify them. Of his TC series he says, "My recent work had been dedicated to the beauties of the aging process—the patina buildup that age, use, and the elements give to the visual world. I am constantly on the lookout for derelict objects and surfaces that excite my eye. The derelict becomes the theme and the variations finalize the makeup of the piece. I attempt to recreate the aged quality by staining, hand rubbing, waxing, weathering, scraping, scratching, burning, fixing, stitching, repainting, and doing what people, elements, and age do to surfaces that make them beautiful. Each piece of art requires a special selection of materials and technical processes, and no single piece is done the same as others."

A FEW CONCLUDING WORDS

There is always the possibility for further exploration and experimentation in working with collage processes. This book presents only a taste of what might be experienced when working with watercolor and collaged papers. And, while it suggests the wide range of personal expression possible with water media and collage, it is not meant to discourage watercolorists from direct painting. To the contrary, it is intended to encourage personal growth and experimentation whatever the medium and to help artists become more aware of design and compositional structure in all their paintings.

I hope that in working your way through this book, you have developed a clearer understanding of the processes involved in constructing paintings in any media. There are alternative ways of working with water media and, by expanding your technical skills and concepts, you can move toward a freedom of expression that is stimulating and dynamic. The more ways you have to express your ideas and visual reactions, the more completely you will be able to respond to the stimulation of your environment. If exploring the possibilities of combining watercolor and collage has opened a few doors for you and encouraged you to try new ways to express your thoughts and visualize your concepts, then compiling this material has been worth the effort.

SELECTED BIBLIOGRAPHY

Your art library should contain books that delve into a variety of subjects, styles, techniques, and media. This bibliography focuses on books that have some relevance to the watercolor and collage technique. The watercolor books, for example, emphasize experimental approaches or deal with textural possibilities. If a book is out of print, it may be available for a library.

BOOKS ON COLLAGE

Brigadier, Anne, *Collage: A Complete Guide for Artists*. New York: Watson-Guptill Publications, 1972.

Brommer, Gerald F., *The Art of Collage*. Worcester, Mass.: Davis Publications, 1978.

Capon, Robin, *Paper Collage*. Newton, Mass.: Charles T. Branford, 1975.

Wolfram, Eddie, *History of Collage*, New York: Macmillan Publishing Company, 1975.

BOOKS ON DESIGN

Graham, Donald W., *Composing Pictures*. New York: Van Nostrand Reinhold Company, 1983.

Henning, Fritz, *Concept and Composition*. Cincinnati: North Light Publishers, 1983.

Loran, Erle, *Cézanne's Composition*. Berkeley and Los Angeles: University of California Press, 1970.

Parramón, J. M., *Composition*. Tucson: H.P. Books/Fisher Publishing, 1981.

BOOKS ON WATERCOLOR

Betts, Edward, *Creative Landscape Painting*. New York: Watson-Guptill Publications, 1978.

Betts, Edward, *Master Class in Watercolor*. New York: Watson-Guptill Publications, 1975.

Blockley, John, *Country Landscapes*. New York: Watson-Guptill Publications, 1982.

Bolton, Richard, *Painting Weathered Textures in Watercolor*. New York: Watson-Guptill Publications, 1982.

Brandt, Rex, *The Winning Ways of Watercolor*. New York: Van Nostrand Reinhold Company, 1973.

Jones, Franklin, *Painting Nature: Solving Landscape Problems*. Westport, Conn.: North Light Publishers, 1978.

Leonard, Elizabeth, *Painting the Landscape*. New York: Watson-Guptill Publications, 1984.

Masterfield, Maxine, *Painting the Spirit of Nature*. New York: Watson-Guptill Publications, 1984.

Quiller, Stephen, and Whipple, Barbara, *Water Media Techniques*. New York: Watson-Guptill Publications, 1983.

Reep, Edward, *The Content of Watercolor*, Revised Edition. New York: Van Nostrand Reinhold Company, 1983.

Shackelford, Bud, *Experimental Watercolor Techniques*. New York: Watson-Guptill Publications, 1980.

Webb, Frank, *Watercolor Energies*. Fairfield, Conn.: North Light Publishers, 1983.

Wood, Robert E., *Watercolor Workshop*. New York: Watson-Guptill Publications, 1974.

INDEX